INSIGHT POCKET GUIDE

Denver
& SUR

Discovery
CHANNEL

APA PUBLICATIONS
Part of the Langenscheidt Publishing Group

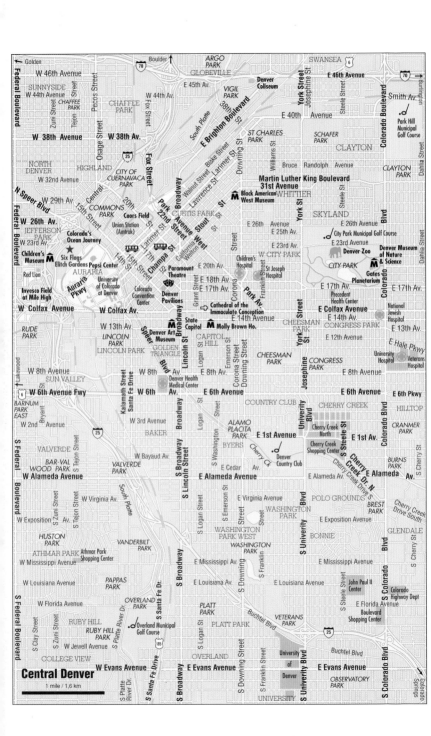

Central Denver

1 mile / 1,6 km

Welcome

This guidebook combines the interests and enthusiasms of two of the world's best-known information providers: Insight Guides, who have set the standard for visual travel guides since 1970, and Discovery Channel, the world's premier source of non-fiction television programming. Its aim is to bring you the best of Denver and its surroundings in the course of six city itineraries and seven out-of-town excursions devised by Donna Dailey, Insight's expert on the Rocky Mountain region.

From its origins as a colorful frontier town to the phenomenal growth of recent years, Denver is one of the most exciting cities in the American West. The itineraries explore the museums, historic buildings, theaters and attractions of downtown Denver, moving on to its beautiful parks and recreation areas. The excursions travel to the popular university town of Boulder, and to the old mining towns of Golden, Georgetown and Central City, and pay due attention to the region's natural attractions, whether you want to look for wildlife in Rocky Mountain National Park, ascend the slopes at Vail or Winter Park, or ride the cog railway to the top of Pike's Peak. The selection of easy day-trips comprises a perfect sampler of the Rockies, both on and off the beaten path.

The itineraries are supported by sections on history and culture, eating out, shopping and nightlife, plus a calendar of special events. At the end of the guide a practical information section covers transport, communications, money, etc, including a list of recommended hotels at all price levels.

Donna Dailey, a travel writer, editor and photographer, lived in Denver for several years. Though wanderlust brought her to London, where she is now based, the beauty of the Rockies continues to lure her back. In this volume she describes not only the important sights, but also the city's fine restaurants, bustling brew pubs, great nightlife, and entertainment. 'People from all over the US come to live in Denver for its climate, its lifestyle, and the outdoor recreation on its doorstep,' she says. 'I was one of them. It's a youthful, vibrant place and, despite its growth, it hasn't lost its casual, fun, friendly air.'

LEISURE ACTIVITIES

CALENDAR OF EVENTS

PRACTICAL INFORMATION

MAPS

CREDITS AND INDEX

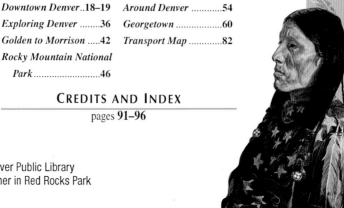

Pages 2/3: Denver Public Library
Pages 8/9: runner in Red Rocks Park

History & Culture

Denver was – and remains – a classic Western boom town. Like its famous California cousin, San Francisco, it was founded during the Gold Rush era of the mid-19th century. But unlike other mining supply towns, Denver has weathered boom-and-bust cycles throughout its history, and its fortunes were tied to underground wealth right up until the present day.

In prehistoric times, the region was a Rocky Mountain Jurassic Park. Dinosaurs thundered over the plains where Denver now stands, and in 1887 the first bones of the great beasts were discovered at Dinosaur Ridge, near the present-day town of Morrison. Among the debris left by the geological upheavals and melting Ice Age glaciers that eroded the ancient mountain range were scattered deposits of gold, nuggets of which were gradually washed down into the mountain stream beds.

Trappers and Traders

In the early 1800s, Arapaho Indians set up camp at the confluence of the Platte River and Cherry Creek, which they named for the wild choke cherry bushes they found there. At times the camp numbered up to 1,500 people, and for half a century they traded buffalo hides and beaver pelts – or 'hairy bank notes' – with the few trappers and traders who ventured west. This peaceful idyll was broken in 1858, when a party of prospectors from Georgia, led by William 'Green' Russell, discovered gold at Cherry Creek. It was only a few grams but, less than a decade after the California gold rush, gold fever was still burning and it didn't take much to spark a new epidemic. In fact, the first Denver gold strike had occurred a year earlier, at a spot known as the 'Mexican Diggings.' But the first city fathers hastily obscured these Hispanic ties, to the point of making it illegal to build with the migrants' usual material, adobe brick.

Russell and his brothers founded the first white settlement on the west side of Cherry Creek and called it Auraria after their hometown – an appropriate name derived from the Latin word for gold. Within the year, three other separate towns were staked out along the creek's banks. Horace Greeley, the publisher from the East who had urged young men to 'go West,' described the settlement as 'a log city of 150 dwellings, not three-fourths completed nor two-thirds inhabited, nor one-third fit to be.'

Then General William H Larimer arrived. He jumped the claim on the land on the east side of the creek and, hoping to gain favor with the Territorial governor, James Denver, renamed it Denver City, unaware that the governor had already resigned. Later, when the Russells returned to Georgia to fight for the South during the Civil War, Larimer declared himself the city's founder. But Larimer also used these strong-arm tactics to the

Left: Buffalo Bill
Right: Straight Crazy, Arapaho man

advantage of his new city. Realizing that fledgling Denver needed links to the civilized world, he bribed a stagecoach company to establish its Rocky Mountain headquarters there.

Rivalry between the settlements festered. William Byers set up his office for the first newspaper, the *Rocky Mountain News*, right in the middle of Cherry Creek so as not to alienate customers in either Denver City to the east or Auraria to the west. But when Golden City, which lay much closer to the gold fields, threatened to usurp the desired position of territorial capital, the sparring townships realized that consolidation was necessary for their survival. Thus, on the night of April 6, 1860, representatives met on the bridge over Cherry Creek, a barrel of whiskey changed hands, and they agreed to become one city: Denver.

Like the gold fields that spawned it, Denver was a gamble. It lacked most of the basic requirements of a city, such as a navigable waterway, and was isolated by hundreds of miles of high treeless plains which were dangerous to cross. Its own gold supply proved paltry, and when a huge find was reported at Central City, the town was nearly deserted as people rushed to the mountains to stake a claim. Some 100,000 fortune hunters flocked to the region in 1859–60, and a year later the federal government established the Colorado Territory. Denver's wild card was its sunny climate. Following a bitter winter in the mountains, people gradually returned and set about making a more modest fortune, with the result that Denver prospered as a trade center and supply town to the mining camps. Miners came down from the hills to drink and gamble. Denverites bet on everything they could think of, and entire town blocks changed hands during card games.

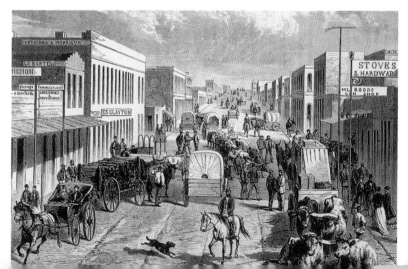

At first, the peaceful Arapaho had welcomed the newcomers. Their chief, Little Raven, greeted them in English, paid cordial visits to their homes, and even invited them to his teepee. Some of Denver's oldest streets, such as Champa, Wewatta, and Wazee, are named after Indian women. The Arapaho watched with concern as more and more settlers built along Cherry Creek, warning them that eventually the creek would flood and sweep everything away.

The land on which Denver grew belonged to the Native Americans, and was recognized by the Fort Laramie Treaty of 1851. Larimer connived to wrest its title from them, and as more and more settlers arrived they became increasingly uneasy about the Arapaho presence among them. In 1861, the Fort Wise Treaty banished them to a reservation to the southeast. Although Little Raven eventually signed, many Arapaho refused.

When Larimer failed to become either mayor of Denver or governor of Colorado, he returned to Kansas, leaving behind a legacy – Larimer Square, Denver's oldest street. Its original buildings were lost in a fire in 1863 that devastated the town. The following year, the Arapaho warnings came true, and a flash flood swept away homes along Cherry Creek killing 20 people. In 1864, skirmishes with the Arapaho and their allies, the Cheyenne, ended in the brutal massacre of over 100 Native Americans at Sand Creek. The survivors, including Little Raven, were eventually forced onto reservations outside the state.

The Denver Pacific Railroad

Despite its hardships, the residents of Denver were determined to survive. By 1865 the city had sturdy brick buildings, four churches, two theaters, and a US mint. But the following year, it seemed Denver's fate was sealed when the Union Pacific Railroad bypassed Colorado and its mountains in favor of a transcontinental route through Cheyenne, Wyoming. Denverites were not so easily defeated. They raised funds and donated labor to build their own railroad, the Denver Pacific, which in 1870 was linked to the Cheyenne line 106 miles (170km) to the north.

Not long after, the Kansas Pacific reached the city from across the plains, and as more rail tracks were built, Denver became the hub of a network that stretched in all directions. The railroad brought gold, minerals, and coal from the mountains to Denver's smelters, agricultural produce from the farming and ranching communities on the plains, and immigrants from Europe. By the turn of the century, 100 trains a day steamed in and out of Union Station. With the railroads in place, Denver was ready for its next big boom: silver.

In 1878, Leadville mines yielded the richest silver strikes in the nation's history, and Denver was once again at the crossroads of a prospecting

Above Left: the last child remaining after the Sandcreek Massacre
Left: Denver, *circa* 1870. **Right:** Leadville mining town

frenzy. Gamblers, gunslingers, and prostitutes filled the saloons on Market and Larimer streets. Legendary lawman Bat Masterson tended bar here. Denver's most famous madame, Mattie Silks, ran an elegant brothel, the House of Mirrors, at 1942 Market Street (now restored as a restaurant). She reputedly fought a topless duel with a rival madame at what is now Commons Park; a poor shot with the gun, she hit her lover by mistake.

'Respectable society' lived up on Capitol Hill. Here, the silver barons built magnificent mansions, some of which survive today. The Denver Tramway Company, headed by John Evans and his son William Gray Evans, built a network of overhead electric streetcars, fueling the growth of the city.

The biggest silver baron of them all was Horace A W Tabor, former mayor of Leadville, who bought up several mining claims including the Matchless Mine, which, at its peak, yielded $100,000 a month. Tabor's fortune grew to $12 million, an enormous amount for the time, and he moved to Denver where he built the opulent Tabor Grand Opera House (now demolished). He doted on his young mistress Baby Doe, and divorced his wife Augusta to marry her. The Tabors scandalized Denver with their extravagance, and their rags-to-riches story is immortalized in John LaTouche's opera, *The Ballad of Baby Doe*. But the story didn't have a happy ending.

In 1893 a crisis struck when half of Denver's 18 banks closed, their resources depleted by backing worthless mining claims. The government repealed the Silver Purchase Act, silver was demonetized, and the price plummeted. As the industry collapsed, Tabor lost his fortune and the couple were poverty-stricken. Horace died in 1899, but Baby Doe struggled on until 1935, when she died alone in a freezing cabin beside the Matchless Mine. Their name lives on in Denver's Tabor Center.

The Silver Panic plunged Denver into a depression, and around 10,000 people left the city. But it was short-lived. A year later, in 1894, the richest gold strike to date was

Above: Denver's notorious Mattie Silks
Left: silver baron Horace Tabor

made at Cripple Creek. Denver's fortunes returned. The boom brought a new crop of *nouveau riche* to the city, such as the 'unsinkable' Molly Brown *(see page 25)*, whose husband J J had made his fortune from the mines in Leadville.

Denver Diversifies

Denver blossomed over the next two decades. The State Capitol building and the Civic Center were erected, grand theaters and hotels were built, and a second major newspaper, the *Denver Post*, was founded.

Some of the most dramatic changes came under the leadership of Robert Speer, who served as mayor from 1904 to 1912, and again from 1916 to 1918. Speer had come to Denver seeking a cure for tuberculosis in the clear air and sunshine. After recovering his health, he set about beautifying the city he now called home. He was a masterful politician with a grand plan for city parks, tree-lined boulevards, and a Civic Center. Under his reign, the city also acquired 20,000 acres (8,000 hectares) of mountain land to fulfill his vision for the Denver Mountain Park System. One of the city's major thoroughfares, Speer Boulevard, which runs along Cherry Creek, is named in his honor.

Denver had learned its lesson from the depression of 1893. To counteract the boom-and-bust cycles of the mining industry, the city set out to diversify its economy. Now, Denver mined the riches of the surrounding plains, railroads hauled livestock and crops into the city, and new industries such as canneries, breweries, stockyards, and leather factories flourished. The Denver Livestock Exchange and the National Western Stock Show were established. One of the city's biggest boosters was the colorful frontier hero, Buffalo Bill *(see page 42)*. By the 1920s, agriculture had replaced mining as Colorado's leading industry.

Despite the building of a municipal airport, Denver's reputation as a sleepy cow town prevailed until well after World War II. During the war, thousands of federal workers were employed at military bases and facilities around the city, while others worked in food production and light manufacturing. After the war, Denver drew newcomers with its good job prospects and fine climate, and the suburbs swelled.

Tourists soon discovered 'the Great Outdoors' that was Denver's back yard – the Rocky Mountains. Spearheaded by the scenic splendor of the Continental Divide, they became a hit with skiers.

From the early 1970s to the mid-1980s, Denver once again rode the wheel of fortune brought by mineral wealth. An Arab oil embargo sparked oil and gas exploration, previously thought uneconomical, and companies came to Denver to set up headquarters for energy-related industries

Right: loan companies flourished

such as shale oil. A host of high-rise office blocks were built to accommodate them, both Downtown and in the suburbs. Denver used this prosperity to build a new Performing Arts Complex and the 16th Street Mall. But the economic bottom fell out when the price of crude oil dropped by $30 a barrel. Denver was hit with another depression, energy companies shut down their operations and the shiny new office buildings stood empty.

Federico Peña, Denver's first Hispanic mayor, elected in 1983, was undaunted. Encouraging Denverites to 'Imagine a Great City,' his term saw the completion of the Platte River Greenway (a 20-mile/32-km public pathway through Downtown), the building of the Colorado Convention Center, and the commitment to the construction of a new Denver international airport. One of the most significant milestones in Denver's growth came in 1988, when the people approved a sales tax increase of 1/10 of a cent to go towards supporting arts and science institutions. In the coming years, Denver residents went to the polls seven times and voted themselves $7 billion in tax increases to fund improvements to their city.

Modern Boom Years

Denver saw tremendous growth at the end of the 20th century. In 1995, the new Coors Field baseball stadium opened in the derelict Lower Downtown and spurred a rapid gentrification of the surrounding streets. With the new Central Library and the expansion of the Convention Center, zoo, and art museum, Denver has at last shed its cow-town image. A new light rail system, which opened in 1994 and expanded in 2000, was eagerly embraced by commuters.

At the start of the 21st century, Denver's population exceeded 2 million. Ironically, many people are relocating here from California in a kind of reverse migration from the Gold Rush days. They are fleeing the high taxes and social problems of the West Coast, the pitfalls of their success. It's a far cry from that creekside camp where General Larimer crossed two cottonwood sticks in 1858, and proclaimed a new city. Larimer wrote to his wife and nine children back home in Kansas, 'Everyone will soon be flocking to Denver for the most picturesque country in the world, with fine air, good water, and everything to make man happy and live to a good old age.' Today, it seems, his vision has come true.

HISTORY HIGHLIGHTS

1851 Arapaho and Cheyenne Indians receive title to land around Cherry Creek in the Treaty of Fort Laramie.

1857 Gold is found on the South Platte River at Mexican Diggings site.

1858 Prospectors from Georgia discover gold at Cherry Creek; the town of Auraria is founded; General Larimer jumps claim on the land to the east of the creek and renames it Denver City.

1859 William Byers starts Denver's first newspaper, the *Rocky Mountain News*.

1860 Denver City and Auraria merge and are renamed Denver.

1861 Colorado Territory is created; the government takes possession of Indian lands in the Treaty of Fort Wise.

1863 A devastating fire destroys much of downtown Denver; telegraph lines connect Denver to the East.

1864 A flash flood in Cherry Creek causes extensive damage; over 100 Native Americans are killed at the Sand Creek Massacre.

1867 Denver becomes the permanent seat of the territorial government.

1870 Denver Pacific Railroad connects with the transcontinental line at Cheyenne, Wyoming.

1871 Denver's first streetcar line is built between Auraria and Five Points.

1876 Colorado becomes the 38th State.

1877 First classes are held at the University of Colorado at Boulder.

1878 A silver strike at Leadville sparks another mining boom. Denver's first telephone lines are laid. Central City Opera House opens.

1881 H A W Tabor builds Tabor Grand Opera House in Denver.

1883 Denver's first electric lights are switched on.

1890 Price of silver soars to over $1 per ounce with the Sherman Silver Purchase Act.

1891 Pike's Peak cog railway begins operation.

1892 *Denver Post* is founded; Brown Palace Hotel opens.

1893 Silver Panic plunges Denver into a depression.

1894 State Capitol is completed; Colorado is the second state, after Wyoming, to give women the vote.

1900 Gold production reaches a peak of $20 million per year at Cripple Creek.

1904–18 Mayor Robert W Speer's 'City Beautiful' program establishes Denver's city and mountain parks.

1906 US Mint in Denver issues first coins; first National Western Stock Show held.

1910 First airplane flight in Denver; first long-distance phone call made to New York City.

1929 Denver Municipal Airport (Stapleton) opens.

1935 Cherry Creek and the Platte River are widened after a disastrous flood.

1967 Many old buildings are torn down to make way for new urban design; Denver Landmark Commission established to protect landmark buildings.

1970s–80s Extensive growth of Denver suburbs.

1973 Following the Arab oil embargo, Denver becomes a center for the oil industry and alternative energy research.

1982 16th Street Mall is completed.

1983–91 Federico Peña becomes Denver's first Hispanic mayor.

1982 Oil crash sends Denver into depression.

1991–2001 Wellington Webb becomes Denver's first African-American mayor.

1994 First light rail line opens from Auraria to Five Points.

1995 Denver International Airport and Coors Field open; new Denver Public Library is completed.

2000–2001 Light rail line is extended; expansion of Convention Center, art museum and other facilities begins.

Left: Denver International Airport has brought great prosperity to the area

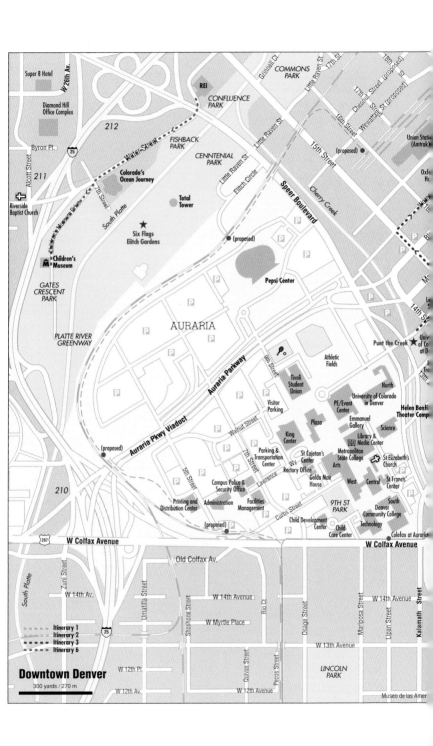

Downtown Denver

300 yards / 270 m

Itinerary 1
Itinerary 2
Itinerary 3
Itinerary 6

City Itineraries

Denver sits at the eastern edge of the Rocky Mountains, in the region of north-central Colorado known as the Front Range. The city's phenomenal growth (its population has increased 23 percent since 1990) has created a sprawling metropolitan region that includes the communities of Aurora, Littleton, Lakewood, Arvada and others. But visitors will find most of the main attractions centrally located, either in downtown Denver or within a 5-mile (8-km) radius of the city center.

The first four itineraries in this guide explore downtown Denver, from the Civic Center to the South Platte River, with its many attractions, restaurants, entertainment and nightlife. The next two itineraries take in City Park, the Botanic Gardens and Cherry Creek. These can all be reached by public transportation, although the latter are more convenient by car.

1. THE CIVIC CENTER *(see map p18–19)*

Many of the city's historic attractions are clustered around the State Capitol. Although all these sights are within easy walking distance, you may need more than one day to see them. This area lacks eating places, but the 16th Street Mall *(see page 25)* is close by.

Book a tour for the Byers-Evans House, tel: 303/620-4933 or the Molly Brown House, tel: 303-832-4092. Any city bus running down Colfax, Lincoln, or Broadway will get you to the Capitol. If you're driving, there's a parking lot opposite the Library at 13th Avenue and Acoma Street.

Start your first day in Denver at one of the most photographed spots in the city – the 18th step leading up to the **Colorado State Capitol** (Mon–Fri 7am–5.30pm; free tours of the interior of the building are given every 45 minutes on weekdays 9am–2.30pm and sometimes on Saturdays in summer) where a plaque tells you that you are standing 'one mile above sea level.' From here there is a magnificent vista across Civic Center Park to the City and County Building, with the peaks of the Rocky Mountains rising in the distance.

Patterned after the national capitol in Washington, DC, Colorado's capitol is built in the shape of a Greek cross with a rotunda in the center and neoclassical features such as Corinthian columns. Construction on the 18-story structure began in 1886, and took 22 years and nearly $3 million. The granite walls, sandstone foundations, and marble floors came from quarries around the state. The crowning glory is the dome, covered with 200 oz (5,670g) of gold leaf, donated by Colorado miners in 1908.

Left: Dome of the Colorado State Capitol. **Right:** a totem pole from Denver Art Museum's Native American collection

The inside of the building is as impressive as the outside, containing ornamental bronzework, stained-glass portraits of historic figures, and murals telling the story of the state's development. The rose onyx for the wainscoting came from Beulah, Colorado and represents the world's entire supply of this rare stone, as the Capitol depleted the only quarry. Four full-time employees have the job of polishing the brass railings and banisters surrounding the rotunda. From the third floor, you can climb 93 steps to the dome's observation deck (Mon–Fri, 9am–3.30pm) for a 360-degree view over Denver.

Head down the steps and straight ahead toward Civic Center Park, passing the red sandstone **Colorado Veterans' Monument**. If you want to detour to the 16th Street Mall for a snack, turn right onto Broadway. On the corner of Colfax and Broadway, the **Pioneer Monument** commemorates the end of the Smoky Hill Trail, an old stage road that brought settlers from the Mis-

souri River to Denver in 1858. The fountain, which depicts a pioneer mother, a miner, and a trapper, was very controversial when it was erected in 1911, and the fourth figure of a Native American which originally topped the statuary was replaced by a statue of frontiersman Kit Carson.

Continue across **Civic Center Park**, with its flower gardens and statues. On the south side is the lifelike **Bronco Buster statue** (1920) by Alexander Proctor. After posing for the artist on a bucking horse, the cowboy model was jailed for horse-stealing. Nearby is the **Greek Theater** (1919) with murals by Alan True, who also painted those in the State Capitol. Built as a venue for band concerts, it is still used for performances and public gatherings. The semi-circular **City and County Building**, which houses government offices, was completed in 1932. The tower clock is dedicated to former mayor Robert Speer, who promoted the building of this and other Denver parks during his terms in the early 20th century.

The US Mint

Behind the City and County Building is the **US Mint** (Mon–Fri 8am–3pm; last Wed of the month opens 9am; free tours are given every 15–20 minutes), entrance on Cherokee Street. This is Denver's most popular attraction and you may have to line up for more than two hours. In summer, the waiting crowd stretches around the block in the burning sun, so the best advice is to arrive early, or bring out your sunscreen and hat.

A mint was established here after the gold discovery in 1858, as it was expensive and difficult to ship gold back East. This building was completed in 1904. As one of only two mints in the country – the other is in Philadelphia – the Denver Mint churns out $6 million in small change every 24 hours. Over 52 million coins of all denominations are produced each day, but around 40 percent of them are pennies. On the tour, which takes 20–30 minutes, you'll see the production line, huge hoppers full of coins, and machines

Above: pioneer monument in Downtown Denver

that spit out 750 golden dollars per minute, faster than a slot machine in Las Vegas. What you won't see is the secret vault in the basement where an estimated $100 billion in solid gold bars are stored, the largest depository of gold bullion in the country after Fort Knox. Instead, walk along the marble walls of the Grand Hallway, past the guard box and Tiffany-style chandeliers. The stunning master chandelier, above the former main entrance on Colfax, is flanked by murals representing Commerce, Mining, and Industry. Exit through the massive brass doors, which weigh around a ton each.

Native American Highlights

Turn right on Colfax and right again on Bannock Street, passing once more through the park. The entrance to the **Denver Art Museum** (Tues–Sat 10am–5pm, Sun 12–5pm, Wed evenings until 9pm; admission fee; free tours are given daily, call 303/640-4433 for current times and topics) is in **Acoma Plaza**, between 13th and 14th avenues. This handsome building, designed by I M Pei, houses an outstanding collection of over 40,000 works of art on seven floors. Highlights include the wonderful collection of Native American art (fourth floor), which features Navajo sand paintings, decorated Plains Indian tepees, and towering totem poles from the northwest coast. The fifth floor has an extensive collection of pre-Columbian ceramics, gold, and tapestries from Central and South America, as well as Spanish Colonial art. Modern and contemporary artworks are displayed on the first floor, while other galleries display European and American art, Asian art, and art of the American West. If you haven't gone to the mall for something to eat, head for Palettes restaurant, which is open during museum hours for lunch, dinner, or buffet meals, and looks out over the courtyard.

Behind the museum on Bannock Street is the historic **Byers-Evans House** (Tues–Sun 11am–3pm; admission fee). Built in 1883 by William Byers, founder of the *Rocky Mountain News*, it was bought

Above: Civic Center Park with Downtown in the background
Right: Native American costume, Denver Art Museum

by businessman William Gray Evans in 1889. The house can only be visited on a half-hour guided tour, which is preceded by a film of nearly equal length detailing the lives of these prominent families. Tour numbers are limited, so arrive early if you haven't booked. The old carriage house contains the Denver History Museum, with displays and video exhibits.

Photographs, Art, Textiles, and Books

Three small galleries opposite the Byers-Evans House on Bannock Street are worth a look. **Camera Obscura** (Tues–Sat, 10am–6pm, Sun 1pm–5pm) showcases vintage and contemporary photographers. **Native American Trading Company** (open Tues–Fri 10am–5pm, Sat 11am–4pm) displays Southwest and Native American Art. Around the corner on 13th Street, **Indigos** (Tues–Sat 11am–5.30pm, Sun 10am–2pm) features traditional and contemporary Asian and American fine art, jewelry, and textiles.

Across the courtyard from the art museum is the **Denver Central Library** (Mon–Wed 10am–9pm, Thur–Sat 10am–5.30pm, Sun 1–5pm; free one-hour tours are given weekdays and Saturday at 11am, Sunday at 2pm), entrance on Broadway. This distinctive, postmodern building, a conglomerate of shapes, angles, and colors, was designed by architect Michael Graves and the Denver firm of Klipp Colussy Jenks DuBois, and opened in 1995. It is the largest library between Chicago and LA, and houses the Western History collection of rare books, maps, and photos. There is a small Western art gallery on the sixth floor, and changing exhibitions on the eighth floor.

The **Colorado History Museum** (Mon–Sat 10am–4.30pm, Sun 12–4.30pm; admission fee) sits opposite the library on Broadway and 13th Avenue. The lower level contains exhibits ranging from Anasazi artifacts from Mesa Verde to memorabilia belonging to silver king Horace Tabor and his wife Baby Doe. The highlight of the museum

Above: a black cowboy at the Colorado History Museum
Left: big red chair outside the Denver Public Library

is the set of miniature dioramas, created between 1933 and 1941, that depict such scenes of frontier life as a river trading post, Cheyenne village, and Pawnee buffalo hunt.

You can walk the six blocks up through the Capitol Hill district to the **Molly Brown House** (Tues–Sat 10am–4pm and Mon June–Aug, Sun 12–4pm; admission fee) at 1340 Pennsylvania Street; if you drive, there are parking meters. Built in 1889, this Queen Anne house was the home of Denver's most famous heroine, Margaret Brown, survivor of the *Titanic* disaster. The stone lions guarding the porch were brought back from her many travels abroad. Costumed guides tell Molly's rags-to-riches story. Although never fully accepted by high society, Molly was self-educated, spoke five languages, and was an avid campaigner for women's and minors' rights. But she was never called Molly in her lifetime – this name was bestowed by the composer of the musical about her life, *The Unsinkable Molly Brown*, because he thought it would be easier to sing. You can only see the house on a guided tour and numbers are limited.

Walk north on Pennsylvania for another block and turn left on Colfax to see the **Cathedral of the Immaculate Conception** (tel: 303/831-7010), completed in 1912. After a peek inside the beautiful interior – light and airy, with a Gothic altarpiece of Carrara marble and Bavarian stained-glass windows – continue down Colfax to return to the State Capitol.

2. THE 16TH STREET MALL *(see map, p18–19)*

A tour along the pedestrian-only 16th Street Mall with its flowers, shops, and cafés, and then to the landmark D&F Tower. Round this off with traditional afternoon tea in the sumptuous Brown Palace Hotel. To enjoy this tour fully, allow at least half a day.

Make reservations for tea at the Brown Palace Hotel, tel: 303/297-3111; the hotel's dress code is 'business casual.' The RTD Civic Center bus station is located at Broadway and 16th Avenue. Buses are free. Denver's light rail line stops right at the mall. Parking lots and meters run along the side streets – the least expensive lie between 15th and Speer, or south of Colfax.

In the early 1980s, a mile-long (1.6 km) section of 16th Street between Broadway and Market Street was bulldozed to create the 16th Street Mall. This popular thoroughfare, which is pedestrian-only save for the free shuttle buses that run frequently along its length, marked the revitalization of downtown Denver. Today the mall is one of the liveliest urban spaces in the United States. In summer, its shady central boulevard blossoms with 50,000 flowers and bubbling fountains,

Right: the 16th Street Mall seen from the D&F Tower

and people lounge on the benches and in pavement cafés or play chess under the trees. The mall's buildings form a timeline of Denver architecture, from 1880s department stores to modern glass-and-steel complexes.

Heading down the Mall

Begin your stroll at the top of the Mall where 16th Street meets **Broadway**. Looking down the Mall, you can see the landmark D&F Tower in the distance, while behind you the top of the State Capitol rises above the office buildings. Turn left on Court Place, passing the entrance to the **Adam's Mark Hotel**; the striking sculpture of ballet dancers out front was erected atop the former ice-skating rink in the old Court House Square. The redstone building at No 1439 is the **Curry-Chucovich House** (1888), the oldest private residence that remains in downtown Denver. Continue to 14th Street, turn right, and right again on Tremont Place to visit the **Trianon Museum and Art Gallery** (Mon–Sat 10am–4pm; tel: 303/623-0739). Its two rooms house a small but delightful collection of 18th- and 19th-century European furniture, paintings, crystal, and objets d'art.

Returning to the Mall, on your left are the **Denver Pavilions**, a two-block-square, open-air complex of stores, restaurants, and movie theaters. These are linked by the Great Wall, a brightly lit, upper-story marquee that straddles Glenarm Place with its signature 'Denver' sign. If you're starting the day here, the Corner Bakery has delicious muffins and scones, while Wolfgang Puck Cafe, Maggiano's Little Italy, and Cafe Odyssey all make great, moderately priced lunch or dinner stops *(see pages 69 and 70)*, but be sure to leave room for afternoon tea.

Afterwards scontinue down the Mall. On the left-hand side, at California Street, look out for the **Denver Dry Building** (1888), which housed the Denver Dry Goods department store for nearly a century. This was the first store in the city to install escalators, and there are plans to reinstate the old tearoom on the sixth floor.

Black Cowboy Heroes

California Street is the stop for the northbound branch of Denver's light rail line. Here, I suggest you make a detour to see the **Black American West Museum** (3091 California Street, May–Sept: daily 10am–5pm; Oct–Apr: Wed–Fri 10am–2pm, Sat–Sun 10am–5pm), which is best reached by light rail and lies just north of Downtown at the final stop at 30th and Downing Street. The museum is housed in the former home of Dr Justina L. Ford who, despite discrimination, established a successful medical practice in Denver between 1902 and 1952. The museum was founded by Paul W Stewart, who as a child had been told there was no such thing as a black cowboy. In fact, nearly a third of the cowboys in the American West were black, and when Stewart grew up, he met one who had led cattle drives at the turn of the 20th century. He then set about compiling this eye-opening collection of artifacts, clothing, photographs, oral histories, and documents that tell the story of black cowboy heroes such as Nat Love (alias Deadwood Dick), frontier scout James Beckwourth, and rodeo riders Bill Pick-

Above: exhibit in the Trianon Museum and Art Gallery
Above Right: the Denver Performing Arts Complex. **Right:** Buskerfest on 16th Street Mall

ett and James Arthur Walker, along with other African-American pioneers who became miners, ranchers, military heroes, and millionaires.

Return by light rail to the corner of Stout and 16th streets, and turn right to continue down the Mall. Cross over Curtis Street and turn left, and as you head toward the **Denver Performing Arts Complex** (DPAC) listen for the Sound Walks – tape recorders positioned in manholes below the sidewalk that surprise passersby with the sudden sounds of cows, pigs, or trains.

Covering four city blocks and encompassing eight theaters *(see page 73)*, the DPAC is the world's largest center of its kind under one roof. This roof is an impressive glass arch, 80 ft (24 meters) high and two blocks long. Theater, musicals, opera, ballet, and concerts are staged here.

Colorado's First Skyscraper

Back on the Mall, at Arapahoe Street the view opens out to the distant mountains. On the right is one of the city's oldest landmarks, the **D&F Tower**. Colorado's first 'skyscraper' is 330 ft (100.58 meters) tall – 375 ft (114 meters) to the top of the flagpole – and when it was built in 1910 it was the tallest building in the country outside New York City. The Italian Renaissance-style structure was modeled after the campanile in Venice's Piazza San Marco. The tower contains its original mechanical clockworks, thought to be the largest of their kind on display in the country. The weights are still wound by hand several times a week. The lobby displaying the clockworks is open to the public.

Behind the tower, think about sitting for a short spell in pleasant **Skyline Park**, a shady plaza built of concrete cubes around a futuristic-looking fountain. Next to one end is the glass-walled **Tabor Center** shopping complex, with

a Visitors Information booth inside. Opposite this is **Writer Square**, another modern development of stores and businesses in the style of an urban village.

The Mall continues on into Lower Downtown, or LoDo (*see Itinerary 3, page 29*). But few can resist stopping to sample one of the 34 different kinds of cheesecake available at the Cheesecake Factory, at the corner of Larimer Street, which also has a lunch and late-night supper menu. Alternatively head back past the tower to the Rock Bottom Brewery at Curtis Street for one of Denver's famous micro-brewed beers. Both restaurants have patios for outdoor dining alongside the Mall.

The Financial District

Retracing your steps to Stout Street, turn left to reach the **Equitable Building**, built in 1892, on the corner of 17th Street. This street has long been Denver's financial district, with many banks and financial institutions located here. Step inside to see the fabulous arched ceiling covered with more than 6 million half-inch (1.3 cm) mosaic tiles. It took 14 men 2½ years to complete the work by hand. The lobby is also adorned with beautiful Tiffany glass windows, five kinds of marble, and a grand brass staircase.

Back on the Mall, the **Masonic Building** (1889) on the corner of 16th and Welton streets was gutted by fire in 1985. To preserve its handsome stone facade, a new steel structure was erected inside. Next door, the decorative gray sandstone Kittredge Building (1891) houses the **Paramount Theater**, Denver's last surviving movie palace, which opened in 1930. Concerts, theater and ballet are staged here, and it is worth seeing a performance if only to view the ornate interior, with red velvet seats, murals, and Art Deco features.

At 56 stories high, the **Republic Plaza Tower** at **Tremont Place** is the tallest building in downtown Denver. The nearby **Wells Fargo Building**, situated on 17th Street, and dubbed the Cash Register Building because of its distinctive shape, appears taller because it stands on a hill but is actually six stories shorter.

Brown Palace Hotel

Turn left at Tremont Place to reach the famous **Brown Palace Hotel**, which commands a triangular plot at Broadway and 17th Street. The tall-spired **Trinity Methodist Church**, opposite, is the oldest in Denver. The hotel was built by Henry Cordes Brown, a carpenter-turned entrepreneur from Ohio who settled in Denver in the 1860s. He donated land nearby for the State Capitol building, then made his fortune selling off the rest of his property on Capitol Hill. But he reserved the three-sided pasture where he grazed his cow to build a grand hotel. The hotel was designed by Frank E Edbrooke, architect of other city landmarks including the State Capitol and the Masonic Building. Nine stories high, it is built of Colorado red granite and Arizona sandstone, in the Italian Renaissance style. Each of the 26 carved stone medallions between the eighth-floor windows depicts a Rocky Mountain animal. The hotel, which took four years and $1.6 million to build, opened in 1892. Then, it had 400 guest rooms that cost from $1 to $4 per night (compared to today's 230 rooms that start at around $200).

Admire the stunning atrium lobby with its massive pillars of white onyx. Have a drink from one of the Art Deco water coolers – the hotel's water comes from its original artesian wells 750ft (228 meters) deep. This grand lobby is the perfect place to end your tour along the Mall. Sink into a chair and prepare to enjoy a sumptuous afternoon tea, accompanied by harp and piano music (daily from 12 noon–4pm).

3. LOWER DOWNTOWN *(see map p18–19)*

This tour takes in the lively streets of LoDo, where Victorian warehouses have been restored to house restaurants, bars, and art galleries.

The daytime walk and a punting trip along Cherry Creek will take just over two hours, but a nighttime visit could last until the wee hours, finishing with a pedicab ride back to your hotel.

If it's a Tuesday through Thursday, book a Punt the Creek trip, tel: 303/893-0750 (optional booking on weekends). The free shuttle down the 16th Street Mall will take you to the starting point at Larimer Square.
It's also an easy walk from the mall's light rail stop. If you're driving, turn onto Market or Wazee streets from Speer Boulevard. From I-25, the closest exits are Speer Boulevard or 20th Street.

LoDo, short for 'Lower Downtown,' is Denver's historic area on the northern edge of Downtown. Though its official boundaries are small – comprising just 26 square blocks from Larimer Street north to Union Station, and from Cherry Creek east to 20th Street and Coors Field – it represents the largest concentration of turn-of-the-20th-century buildings in America. During that era, LoDo was a busy commercial center, full of large warehouses and showrooms which were the forerunners of department stores. Denver

Above: Denver school boys pose for the camera
Left: Brown Palace Hotel, downtown. **Right:** LoDo sign

was then a major railroad center, and the warehouses held goods that were distributed throughout the Rockies and the West.

The subsequent downtown development boom stopped at Larimer Street, leaving a blighted area to the north. Less than 10 years ago, LoDo was a no-go area after dark, a haven for drug-dealers and down-and-outs. All that changed in 1995 with the opening of the 50,000-seat Coors Field baseball stadium at Blake and 20th streets. Suddenly thousands of people were trooping through LoDo on their way to the games, and their potential custom sparked the regeneration of the neighborhood.

LoDo Transformation

The old Lower Downtown warehouses have been gutted and transformed. Bars and restaurants with exposed brick walls, hard-wood floors and large windows have been installed at street level while upper floors have been turned into desirable lofts and apartments. Within five years, LoDo went from having no residents (at least, not tax-paying ones) to 5,000, a figure that will double when

further development plans are complete. Today, LoDo is the trendiest area of the city, Denver's nightlife capital with around 90 bars, restaurants, nightclubs, and brew pubs. On most nights, especially in summer, LoDo resembles a huge outdoor party with people strolling the streets from one bar or club to the next. More than 30 art galleries have also staked space here, displaying a variety of styles from Native American art to contemporary works by Colorado artists. Most are open late (until 9pm) and hold special events on the first Friday of each month; call 303/321-1510 for information.

LoDo does not have any tourist sights per se. Its appeal lies in its atmosphere, which is visually attractive by day but most vibrant at night. The following route notes a few LoDo landmarks, but the best way to explore this district is simply to stroll through the streets and discover your own favorite haunts. As you wander past its handsome facades, look for the 33 bronze plaques attached to the walls which tell their history and that of the characters who once lived here and gave Denver its colorful legacy.

Before you set off, a word about the brewpubs. More beer is brewed in Denver than in any other American city. The first permanent structure in Denver was a saloon, so it is not surprising that today there are 15 brewpubs and microbreweries in the downtown area. By definition, a brewpub produces less than 15,000 barrels of beer a year and also serves food. It is generally housed in premises where you can actually see the large stainless steel tanks in which the beer is made. In most cases the beer is only served fresh from the keg.

Above: Punting in Cherry Creek, LoDo. **Right:** Larimer Square in LoDo

If the brewpub bottles the beer, it technically becomes a microbrewery. A brewpub usually has five or six beers on tap ranging from light beers to dark stouts, which sport such names as Fat Tire, Railyard Ale and Sagebrush Stout. Most offer 'samplers' or 4oz (0.1-liter) tastings.

Denver's Oldest Street

Begin your tour in **Larimer Square**, which runs along Larimer Street between 14th and 15th streets. On the edge of LoDo, it was the first area to be restored when 18 Victorian buildings were saved from demolition in the 1970s and converted into a fashionable shopping and dining area. Denver's oldest street is named for General William H Larimer, who jumped a claim by earlier settlers in 1858 to establish the townsite which he named 'Denver' *(see page 11)*. The **Granite Building** at 1228 15th Street stands on the site where he built his log cabin, using coffin lids for doors. Western legends such as Bat Masterson and Buffalo Bill Cody also claimed a Larimer Street address during their well-documented lifetimes.

On the north side of the street at No 1445 is the Square's trendiest hangout, **The Market**, where you can survey the scene over a coffee, pastry, sandwich or ice cream. Horse-drawn carriages leave from Larimer Square for trips through LoDo or up the 16th Street Mall. At the end of Larimer Street where it meets Cherry Creek you can buy a ticket to **Punt the Creek** (June–Aug: Tues–Sun 4pm–dusk). This is a fun way to hear about Denver's beginnings as you glide along Cherry Creek to Confluence Park *(see Itinerary 6, page 38)* in a flat-bottomed boat, or punt, propelled by a long pole. The trip takes about an hour and 15 minutes, and punts leave every 10 minutes.

From Larimer Square, walk down 15th Street, which is lined with bars and eating places, into the heart of LoDo. Turn right at Wazee Street. At the corner with 17th Street is the historic **Oxford Hotel** *(see page 84)*. It was built in 1891 during Colorado's silver boom to provide top-quality accommodations near the railroad station. Its architect, Frank E Edbrooke, also built Denver's Brown Palace Hotel, and designed the Oxford around a light well so that all of the interior rooms have natural light. Step into the lobby, furnished with French and English antiques, to admire its elegant Victorian decor. The piano is from the old Tabor Grand Opera House (now demolished). Off the lobby is the atmospheric Cruise Room bar, an Art-Deco delight

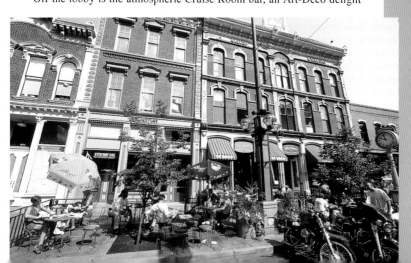

built in the 1930s. This long, narrow room has red lighting, black booths and hand-carved panels that portray the end of Prohibition.

Turn left out of the hotel and continue one block on 17th Street to **Union Station**, which forms the northern boundary of LoDo. Built in 1881, it still serves as a railroad terminal for Amtrak *(see page 79)*, and is the departure point for the weekend Ski Train to Winter Park *(see Excursion 4, page 55)*. Though modern restaurants and other facilities have been added to the wings, the central waiting room is charmingly early 20th-century, with arched windows and tall-backed wooden benches with overhead reading lights.

Bookstores & Brewpubs

The station faces Wynkoop Street, which contains many LoDo highlights. On the corner with 16th Street is the Downtown branch of the **Tattered Cover Book Store** *(see pages 35 & 66)*, complete with cosy armchairs and reading nooks. Colorado's first brewpub, the **Wynkoop Brewing Company**, occupies the beautiful turn-of-the-20th century J S Brown Mercantile at 18th Street and Wynkoop. This was LoDo's first major enterprise, founded in 1988 by LoDo pioneer John Hickenlooper who saw the area's potential well before the completion of the baseball stadium. Today Wynkoop is one of the largest brewpubs in the country, with a restaurant, a comedy club, and a huge pool hall. Stop here to try the German-style Railyard Ale, or one of their many other specialty beers.

Another striking brick building, the **Ice House**, stands opposite the brewery on Wynkoop. It was built in 1903 as a cold storage plant for the Littleton Creamery, and is said to have stored furs and even corpses as well as dairy

Above: Colorado Rockies baseball game at Coors Field
Right: Union Station entrance sign

products. The somewhat spooky basement level lends credibility to the tale, but otherwise the building sports a smart lobby, good restaurants and a deli.

Continue along Wynkoop to **Coors Field** (tours are given Mon–Fri at 10am, 12 noon and 2pm; admission fee). Denver's $215 million baseball stadium, home of the Colorado Rockies baseball team, opened for the 1995 season. It was built to resemble the classic ballparks of the 1940s and '50s, with a brick facade that blends in with the surrounding neighborhood. The inside is designed like an old ballpark, but with modern amenities and seating.

The stadium also has its own brewpub, **Sandlot Brewing Company**, built right into Coors Field. It's not surprising that it's owned by the giant brewery which sponsored the stadium, but it features hand-crafted small batch beers. Nearby is **Breckenridge Brewery**, opposite the stadium at 2220 Blake. Four of its beers are sold throughout the region, but you can also try Avalanche Ale and other favorites straight from the keg. If you've imbibed one too many, take a pedicab – Denver's version of a rickshaw – back to your hotel.

To continue your walking tour, head east on 20th Street to **Sakura Square**, a small Japanese enclave. During World War II, when people of Japanese descent faced increasing hostility in the US, Governor Ralph Carr welcomed them to Colorado. A bronze bust in his honor stands in the square. The Pacific Mercantile Company, which sells Asian foods and gifts, was founded here in 1942. Adjoining it is a small museum of contemporary art. Larimer Street borders one side of the square and will take you back to Larimer Square.

4. DENVER BOTANIC GARDENS
AND CHERRY CREEK *(see map p36)*

This half-day tour includes a fragrant walk through Denver Botanic Gardens, followed by a shopping spree at nearby Cherry Creek.

The Botanic Gardens, on bus route 24, are 10 minutes' drive east of downtown Denver with a parking lot between Josephine and York streets. The Cherry Creek shopping district lies on either side of 1st Avenue between University and Colorado boulevards. Bus routes 1, 2, 3, 24, 3 Ltd and 83 Ltd service Cherry Creek.

Coupled with Cheesman Park which adjoins it to the west, **Denver Botanic Gardens** (Oct–Apr: daily 9am–5pm; May-Sept: Wed–Fri 9am–5pm , Sat–Tues 9am–8pm; admission fee) is another of the central city's emeralds. It is rated as one of the top botanic gardens in the country and features 23 acres (9.3 hectares) of flowers, trees, and exotic plants, with more than 15,000 species.

The humid, misty Tropica Botanica collection is housed in the only major tropical conservatory in the Rockies. For a great view, ascend to the overhead decks via the elevator

Right: Monet Garden, Denver Botanical Gardens

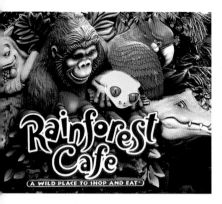

disguised in a banyan tree. Outdoors, plants from all over the world are featured in 30 gardens, including such delights as a Japanese Garden complete with teahouse, the Flytrap Feast with carnivorous plants, and the Monet Garden with flowers and waterlilies inspired by the canvases of French Impressionist Claude Monet. The rock alpine garden covers an acre and may be the finest in the country. Colorado plants also take pride of place, and the gardens feature rare and endangered species of wild-flowers, sacred plants used by Native Americans on the Colorado plateau, unusual flora from the dryland mesa, and an heirloom garden with favorite plants brought to Colorado by pioneers. Special events are held throughout the year. In summer there are sunrise fitness walks, sunset garden strolls, and a concert series. At Christmastime lights are strung in the shape of flowers.

Non-Stop Shopping

Take York Street south to reach Cherry Creek. Turn left on 1st Avenue and on the right is the enormous **Cherry Creek Shopping Center** (Mon–Fri 10am–9pm, Sat 10am–7pm, Sun 11am–6pm). There's free parking on the eastern end of the mall, not far from Foley's department store. This smartly designed mall opened in 1990 as the only world-class shopping center in the region, with upscale department stores such as Neiman Marcus, Saks Fifth Avenue, and Lord & Taylor. Tiffany, Burberry, and Louis Vuitton are also among the 160 stores, but there are other specialty retailers where the goods won't break the bank. The mall has become an attraction in its own right; the Denver Convention and Visitors Bureau has an information booth here. There are several good restaurants *(see page 69)*.

By contrast, **Cherry Creek North**, opposite the mall, is an outdoor shopping area filling 16 blocks from 1st to 3rd avenues and from University Boulevard

to Steele Street. Here, art galleries, boutiques, gift shops and salons are dotted along tree-lined streets. It's a leisurely place for browsing, with many restaurants and coffee shops *(see page 69)*. On a hot day, try a cool **Jamba Juice** (200 Fillmore, and branches all over town), a range of high-energy fruit slushes. **Fillmore Plaza** is a pedestrianized block between 1st and 2nd avenues. In summer, you may want to take in one of the weekend jazz concerts or an outdoor movie screening.

At 1st Avenue and Milwaukee Street is the famous **Tattered Cover Book Store** (Mon–Sat 9am–11pm, Sun 10am–6pm). With more than half a million volumes on four floors, this beloved bookshop may well stock that hard-to-find title you've been looking for. It features comfortable armchairs and cosy reading nooks, author readings and book signings, nationwide newspapers and foreign magazines, a coffee shop on the ground floor and a fourth-floor restaurant and bar *(see pages 32 & 66)*.

5. CITY PARK *(see map p36)*

City Park is an oasis in the center of Denver, containing the zoo and the Museum of Nature and Science, with an IMAX theater. You can see everything in the park in one long day, or combine a couple of the sights with a stroll for a leisurely half-day outing.

If you're driving from Downtown, take 17th Avenue east to York Street. The park lies between York and Colorado Boulevard, where there is also an entrance to the Museum of Nature and Science.

With 200 parks within the city limits and another 20,000 acres (8,000 hectares) in the nearby mountains, Denver has the largest city park system in the United States. One of its oldest parks is **City Park**, transformed in 1881 from a field of sagebrush into a 314-acre (127-hectare) haven of green lawns and rose gardens. Its central feature is a lake enclosed by tall trees; all around are grassy picnic spots and paths for bicycling, skating, and walking. In summer you can rent paddleboats on the lake. On the west shore, the restored 19th-century City Park Pavilion serves as a bandstand for local musicians. There are also horseshoe pits and tennis courts in the northwest corner of the park.

Denver Zoo

The main entrance to the **Denver Zoo** (daily Apr–Sept: 9am–6pm; Oct–Mar:10am–5pm; admission fee), which lies within the park boundaries, is on 23rd Avenue. The zoo had humble beginnings in 1896 when an American black bear called Billy Bryan was tethered to a tree in City Park. Its landmark Bear Mountain, built in 1918, was the country's first naturalistic habitat without bars. Today the zoo is Colorado's top cultural attraction, home to nearly 4,000 animals representing some 685 species. Wildlife conservation remains a top priority at the zoo, with many programs dedicated to protecting endangered species.

Top Left: Rainforest Café, Cherry Creek Shopping Center
Left: in the Botanical Gardens. **Right:** Komodo Dragon, the Zoo

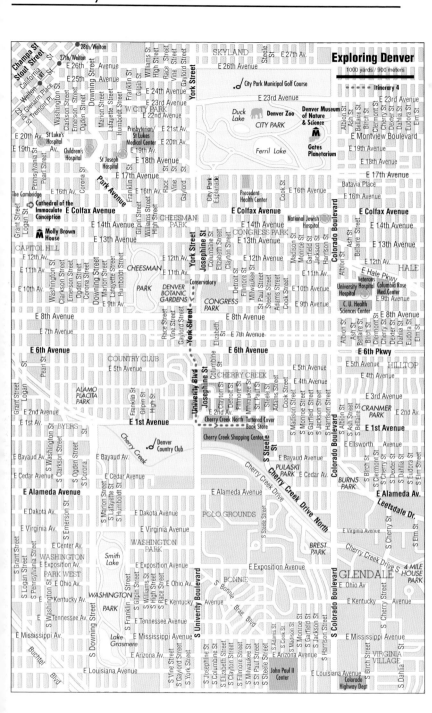

Exploring Denver

Among the zoo's highlights are the Primate Panorama, covering acres of re-created natural habitats for 29 species of primates from lemurs to lowland gorillas, the Tropical Discovery exhibit which simulates a rain forest, and the Dragons of Komodo *(see picture on page 35)*. The zoo train rides are also fun for children.

History of the Planet Earth
The **Denver Museum of Nature and Science** (daily 9am–5pm, Tues until 7pm in summer) is situated at the eastern end of City Park, with the entrance on Montview off Colorado Boulevard. This is the fifth-largest natural history museum in the United States. To see one of the main highlights of the museum, proceed straight up to the third floor to embark on a fascinating 'Prehistoric Journey,' taking you back 3.5 billion years to the beginnings of life on earth. The exhibit traces the development of plants and animals using reconstructed fossil sites from actual locations and placing them in realistic settings.

This leads on to everyone's favorite display, the museum's 12 dinosaur skeletons, which include an 80-ft (24-meter) long Diplodocus, and an Allosaurus and Stegosaurus engaged in battle. In the next room is a diorama of a scary beast called a Dinohyus, nicknamed the 'terminator pig', depicted stalking its prey on the Nebraska woodland around 20 million years ago.

Another major exhibit is the Hall of Life, with hands-on displays relating to such topics as the anatomy and the five senses. It includes more than 80 dioramas depicting wildlife from each of the five continents, as well as Egyptian mummies, totem poles, and tepees.

The museum is also home to the **Gates Planetarium**, which presents shows about the stars, and an **IMAX theater**, which usually shows movies on adventure themes or the natural world.

For refreshments, including plenty of options for children, stop by the T-Rex Cafe and Deli, located near the museum shop.

Above: dinosaur skeletons on the 'Prehistoric Journey' in the Denver Museum of Nature and Science

6. THE SOUTH PLATTE VALLEY *(see map p18–19)*

A world-class aquarium, a thrilling roller coaster ride, a streetcar and a ski mountain are some of the kid-friendly attractions along the South Platte River. Choose among the activities here, as most take a few hours.

You may want to pack a picnic and a swimsuit. You will also need to arrange for a car. To access Confluence Park, Colorado's Ocean Journey, and the Children's Museum, take 15th Street from Downtown and turn left (south) on Platte Street, or take the 23rd Avenue exit from I-25. Elitch Gardens has an exit off Speer Boulevard. RTD bus No 10 runs to Ocean Journey.

The South Platte Valley is a sprawling area that lies northwest, roughly between Speer Boulevard and I-25. Denver's first pioneers settled here along the South Platte River, deeming its muddy waters 'too thin to plow, too thick to drink.' For many years the land surrounding this stretch was an industrial wasteland, for the river had flooded several times in Denver's history, causing extensive damage. In the 1990s, however, a new river channel was dug to prevent flooding, enabling the valley to be developed for recreation. Bicycle paths now run along the South Platte for 12 miles (19km) through the city. A stable water flow allows a stretch of the river to be used for kayaking and rafting. There are picnic areas and wetlands with native plants and wildlife along the banks – including beavers.

Running the Rapids

Start at **Confluence Park**, below 15th and Platte streets, where Cherry Creek meets the South Platte River. In 1858, the first settlers panned for gold here. Most were unsuccessful and moved on, but a few stayed to found the early city. Today it is a popular spot for kayakers who run the rapids and families who picnic along the banks and swim. **Commons Park**, a new 30-acre (12-hectare) green space with a promenade, is under construction nearby.

The mammoth **REI** sporting goods store above the park is worth checking out *(see page 65).* It features a 45-ft (14-meter) high rock-climbing wall and a mountain bike track. Next door, on 15th Street, **My Brother's Bar** is a long-established Denver watering hole that serves some of the best burgers in town.

Continue west on Water Street to **Colorado's Ocean Journey** (daily late May–early Sept: 9am–6pm; rest of the year: 10am–6pm; admission fee). This

aquarium harbors around 300 species of fish, birds, and mammals. The tanks are installed amid a series of environments that simulate two river journeys on opposite sides of the world – one along the Colorado River, the other along Indonesia's Kampar River. Though both start at 12,000 ft (3,658 meters) above sea level and end in the Pacific Ocean, you will pass through two entirely different sets of ecosystems. A favorite spot is the 'Flash Flood' where 2,500 gallons (11,365 liters) of water come rushing down a canyon. The exhibits encompass a range of aquatic life, including sharks, jellyfish, river otters, and two Sumatran tigers who love to swim.

Family Fun

Just beyond this is the **Children's Museum** (Tues–Fri 9am–4pm and Mon in summer, Sat–Sun 10am–5pm; admission fee). This is a great museum for families, with interactive exhibits and activities such as a Science Lab and Children's Theater. Its famous **Kids' Slope** is a year-round, plastic ski mountain where youngsters can take their first run. You can eat at the Pepsi Riverside Cafe on the lower level of the aquarium, or bring a picnic lunch to enjoy in the park alongside the Children's Museum.

Outside the museum is a stop for the **Platte Valley Trolley** (daily 11am–5pm in summer, hours vary fall–spring; tel: 303/458-6255; admission fee). This open-top streetcar is a replica of those operated by the Denver Tramway Company before World War I. It follows a scenic route along the South Platte River, on part of the old 1890s railroad track. It has five stops, including one at REI. The trip takes 20 minutes.

From the bicycle path there is a fine view of **Six Flags Elitch Gardens** (open May–early Sept: 10am–10pm, Sept–Apr: call 303/595-4386 for hours; admission fee) across the river. It is best reached off Speer Boulevard via the turn-off at Elitch Circle. The amusement park was created by John and Mary Elitch at their orchard in northwest Denver in 1890, and was moved here in 1995. It features 48 thrill rides. Admission is steep, but the rides are included in the entrance fee.

Near Elitch's, the soda-can-shaped building is the **Pepsi Center**, a top concert venue and home of Denver's hockey and basketball teams.

The small but highly regarded **Museo de las Americas** (861 Santa Fe Drive, tel: 303/571-4401; Tues–Sat 10am–5pm, admission fee) is located in a Hispanic neighborhood just south of downtown and is best reached by car. Dedicated to Latino life, art, culture and history in the Americas, it hosts changing exhibitions. The two back rooms display art from the museum's permanent collection, which ranges from paintings, *bultos* (wooden statues) and other images of devotion from the Spanish Colonial period, to contemporary works.

Left: Cherry Creek, Confluence Park
Right: 'The Mind Eraser,' Six Flags Elitch Gardens amusement park

Excursions

1. GOLDEN *(see map p42)*

The town of Golden, Denver's westernmost area, has many attractions from its Victorian main street and Coors brewery to nearby Red Rocks Amphitheater and the grave of Buffalo Bill. Finish the day with a concert or a Mexican meal.

If it's summer, call to see if tickets are available for that evening's concert at Red Rocks Amphitheater, tel: 303/458-4850. Golden is about a 30-minute drive from central Denver and the easiest way is to take I-70 west, which has several exits for Golden. You can also take 6th Avenue/Highway 6 or Highway 40, which is the same as West Colfax Avenue.

Golden was founded at the mouth of Clear Creek Canyon around the same time as Denver, in 1859, when gold was discovered in the stream that runs through town. It was named for an early prospector with the appropriate moniker of Thomas L Golden who had set up camp near the creek a year earlier. The young towns were rivals for several years. Golden served as the capital of the Colorado Territory from 1862 to 1867 before losing the distinction to Denver in a highly contested vote. Today this town of around 15,000 residents is one of the fastest growing in the region. New high-tech industries are setting up shop here, alongside major employers such as Coors Brewery and the venerable Colorado School of Mines, founded in 1874 for the development of mineral sciences and engineering.

America's First Saint

Head west from Denver on I-70 and take Exit 259, which also leads south to Red Rocks Park *(see page 44)*. Follow signs for Highway 40 West and the **Mother Cabrini Shrine** (daily late May–early Sept: 7am–8pm; rest of the year: 7am–5pm), reached by a pretty 3-mile (5-km) drive up a winding mountain road. It honors St Frances Xavier Cabrini, America's first saint, who founded a missionary order of sisters in 1880. Pilgrims visit the grotto chapel and spring, and climb the 373 steps to a 22-ft (6.5-meter) tall statue of Christ. At the top are panoramic views over Denver.

Return to Highway 40, which parallels I-70, and turn right. The turn-off for Buffalo Bill's Grave and Museum is off this road to the right (or via Exit 256 from I-70). An optional detour is to continue west on this road for a few more miles to the I-70 overpass (Exit

Left: Red Rocks Ampitheater, Morrison
Right: Stations of the Cross, Golden

254) which leads to **Genesee Park**, a good place to see herds of elk and bison. Denver's **buffalo herd** is directly descended from the last wild buffalo herd in America, which was protected in Yellowstone National Park. Conservationists were concerned that a natural disaster there could result in the extinction of the species, so in 1914 a small herd was donated to Denver Mountain Parks. Numbering around 30 buffalo, the herd roams back and forth between north and south pastures beneath the highway. Take the Genesee exit, also marked **Buffalo Overlook**, off of I-70 to reach the viewing areas. On winter mornings, the city puts out feed for the animals on the north side.

Buffalo Bill

Head back east and take the turn-off for Lookout Mountain Road (Exit 256) which leads to **Buffalo Bill's Grave and Museum** (Tues–Sun, May–Oct: 9am–5pm, Nov–Apr: 9am–4pm; admission fee). William F Cody (1846–1917) was one of the most famous figures of the Old West. He was a cattle herder, Pony Express rider, gold miner and Army scout, but it was his skill as a buffalo hunter that earned him his nickname, ''Buffalo Bill.' A celebrity by the age of 27, Cody acted in melodramas with Wild Bill Hickok. In 1883 he launched his Wild West Show, whose large company included the sharpshooter Annie Oakley as well as Chief Sitting Bull and other Indians whom, ironically, he had once fought and helped to move out to reservations. The popular shows strove to portray a sentimental vision of the Wild West and Cody became an icon as people memorialized the vanishing frontier.

Cody died in Denver in January 1917, causing a controversy that persists to this day. The towns of Cody, Wyoming, which he had founded, and North Platte, Nebraska, where he had a ranch, both wanted the body and disputed Denver's claim that Buffalo Bill had expressed a wish to be buried on Lookout Mountain. He was finally interred here four months later, but the battle over his burial site continued and several years on the National Guard was called in to protect the grave from robbers. You can visit the grave, now anchored beneath concrete, which lies up a shady path from the museum.

Golden to Morrison

The museum presents an entertaining look at Buffalo Bill's life as a frontiersman and showman, with guns, costumes, memorabilia, and posters from his Wild West shows. Adjoining the museum is an observation deck with stunning views.

As you exit the museum, turn left

excursions

and wind your way slowly down the sharp but scenic curves of Lookout Mountain Road into **Golden** below. At the bottom, cross over Highway 6 and continue straight ahead on 19th Street, also called the Lariat Trail. Turn left on Washington Street which brings you into the town's historic business district. The blocks between 13th and 10th streets are lined with handsome brick Victorian buildings, housing gift shops, art galleries, bars, and restaurants beneath the wooden arcades. There are bright flower beds and benches on every corner. More historic buildings from the 1860s line 12th Street, including the **Astor House Museum** (open Tues–Sat 10am–4.30pm, admission fee), a frontier boarding house with period furnishings.

There are several pleasant restaurants to choose from for lunch *(see page 72)* but for a bit of nostalgia try **The Golden Ram** (Mon–Sat until 3pm, Sun until 2pm), round the corner on 13th Street in the Foss Building. It began as a soda fountain in the Foss General Store, and now serves home-cooked meals, burgers, sandwiches, and great breakfasts.

Golden has several small museums worth visiting. These include the **Rocky Mountain Quilt Museum** (1111 Washington Avenue; opening hours vary); the **Golden Pioneer Museum** (923 10th Street, open Mon–Sat 10am–4.30pm); and the **Colorado Railroad Museum** (17155 West 44th Avenue, open daily 9am–5pm; admission fee). Golden's biggest draw, however, is the **Coors Brewing Company** (Mon–Sat 10am–4pm, guided tours every 15 minutes), located three blocks east of the center on 12th Street. German immigrant Adolph Coors founded his brewery beside Clear Creek in 1873. Today, with production of more than 17 million barrels a year, this is the largest single brewery in the world. The first half-hour of the free 90-minute tour takes you through the entire brewing process, from germinating barley to bot-

Above: Old West murals, Foss General Store, Golden
Right: sampling lounge, Coors Brewery, Golden

tling. You can sample the beer (proof that you're 21 and of legal drinking age is required) and decide for yourself if the popular brew is to your liking.

South of Golden

If you've got children in tow, leave Golden on 6th Avenue toward the interstate and follow signs for **Heritage Square** (open 11am–8 or 9pm; admission free, charge for rides). Otherwise, there's little to interest adults in this cotton-candy amusement park.

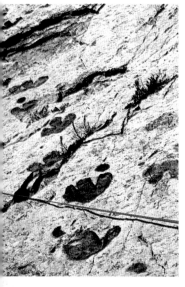

Pass the entrances to I-70 and continue south to the turn-off for **Red Rocks Amphitheater**. Denver's finest concert venue took 300 million years to build, carved by nature between two 400-ft (122-meter) high red sandstone monoliths known as Ship Rock and Creation Rock. It has 9,000 seats and superb acoustics. Since its opening in 1936, it has hosted the world's top performers, from composer Igor Stravinsky to The Beatles to U2, who used it as a backdrop for their music video *Under a Blood Red Sky*. A performance here under the stars is magical, so do try and attend a performance during your stay. Alternatively, you can visit free of charge any time of the year, although the premises close at 4pm on event days. There are views over the plains to the distant Denver skyline 15 miles (24 km) away.

The amphitheater is surrounded by the 640-acre (259-hectare) **Red Rocks Park**, with a nature trail posted with signs explaining the geology of the area. It was once the beach of a great inland sea that covered much of Colorado. When the Rocky Mountains were formed, this beach was compressed into soft red rocks and pushed upwards into the formations you see today.

The 'Great Dinosaur Rush'

Opposite Red Rocks on West Alameda Parkway is **Dinosaur Ridge** (Mon–Sat 9am–4pm, Sun 12–4pm), the site where the world's first large dinosaur bones were discovered by a schoolteacher in 1887. These included stegosaurus, allosaurus, and brontosaurus bones. The discovery sparked the 'great dinosaur rush' as scientists poured into the area looking for more fossil sites. Many dinosaur bones are still trapped in the sandstone on the west side of Dinosaur Ridge. On the east side, more than 300 dinosaur footprints are preserved. These can be seen along a path marked with interpretive signs. The Visitor Center has displays about the site, while the Natural History Museum in nearby Morrison has original bones from the first dinosaur dig.

Continue south on Highway 26 to **Morrison**. This delightful little town has a few small shops and eateries along its one main street, Bear Creek Avenue. Have a beer or some good Mexican food at the **Morrison Inn**, where historic photos grace the walls, before returning to Denver.

Above: giant footprints, Dinosaur Ridge. **Right:** in the Rocky Mountain National Park

excursions

2. ROCKY MOUNTAIN NATIONAL PARK *(see map p46)*

If you have only one day to see the Rocky Mountains, spend it in Rocky Mountain National Park. The highest continuous road in America, Trail Ridge Road, runs through this park. You'll need 3–4 hours, including stops, to drive it, but it's best to allow a full day, especially if you want to picnic or hike on the trails. The park is open year round, but Trail Ridge Road is closed in winter.

Phone park headquarters, tel: 970/586-1206, to check seasonal hours and weather conditions before setting out. There are two main gateways into the park, which is located 71 miles (114km) northwest of Denver. Take US Highway 36 through Boulder to Estes Park. The scenic Peak to Peak Highway (Highways 72 and 7 north from Nederland), will also take you to the eastern entrances. To reach the western gateway, take I-70 west, then at Empire head north on Highway 40 through Winter Park, Granby, and Grand Lake. US 34 (Trail Ridge Road) runs east–west through the park.

Encompassing 415 sq miles (1,075 sq km) of wilderness, **Rocky Mountain National Park** (admission fee, good for seven days) contains some of the most awesome scenery in Colorado. Its lofty peaks and deep valleys, carved by glaciers during the Ice Age, were summer hunting grounds for the Ute and Arapaho Indians before the Europeans arrived. The region attracted tourists early on, following the English traveler Isabella Bird's visit to Estes Park in 1873 and the publication of her book, *A Lady's Life in the Rocky Mountains.* In the early 1900s, another eloquent writer and naturalist, Enos Mills, conducted nature trips and lobbied for the area to be preserved as the country's 10th national park. President Woodrow Wilson declared it so in 1915.

Before setting out you can pick up maps and information at the park visitor centers, located near the entrances (open 8am–6 or 8pm in summer). There are other visitor centers within the park. The only snack bar is at the Trail Ridge store, adjacent to the Alpine Visitor Center. Bring a picnic if you're coming for the day, or there are plenty of restaurants and shops in Estes Park and Grand Lake. The park can get very busy in high season, so arrive early to avoid having traffic congestion spoil your views.

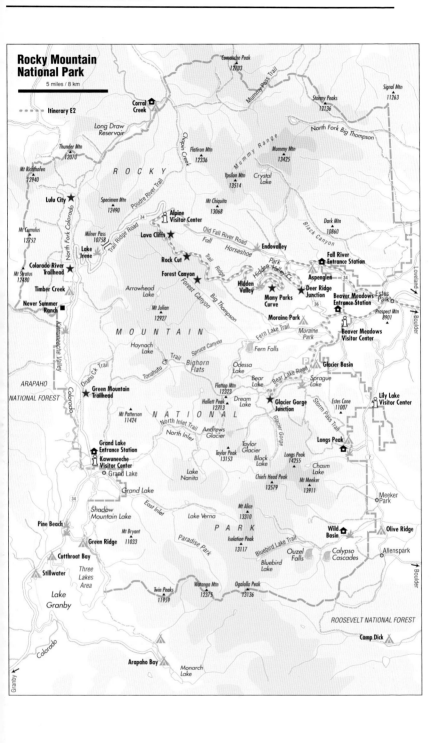

Rocky Mountain National Park

5 miles / 8 km

- - - Itinerary E2

Corral Creek

Long Draw Reservoir

Thunder Mtn 12070

Mt Richthofen 12940

R O C K Y

Lulu City

Specimen Mtn 12490

Mt Cumulus 12752

Milner Pass 10758

Colorado River Trailhead

Mt Stratus 12480

Timber Creek

Never Summer Ranch

Lake Irene

Trail Ridge Road

Poudre River Trail

Alpine Visitor Center

Lava Cliffs

Rock Cut

Forest Canyon

Arrowhead Lake

Mt Julian 12927

Mt Chiquita 13068

Old Fall River Road

Fall

Horseshoe

Trail Ridge

Big Thompson

Comanche Peak 12703

Mummy Pass Trail

Stormy Peaks 12136

Signal Mtn 11263

North Fork Big Thompson

Flatiron Mtn 12336

Chapin Creek

Mummy Range

Mummy Mtn 13425

Ypsilon Mtn 13514

Crystal Lake

Dark Mtn 10860

Black Canyon

Endovalley

Park Valley Cr.

Hidden Valley

Hidden Valley

Many Parks Curve

Deer Ridge Junction

Moraine Park

Fall River Entrance Station

Aspenglen

Beaver Meadows Entrance Station

Estes Park

Prospect Mtn 8901

Loveland

Boulder

M O U N T A I N

Haynach Lake

Onahu Ck Trail

Green Mountain Trailhead

Mt Patterson 11424

Tonahutu

Trail

Spruce Canyon

Bighorn Flats

Fern Lake Trail

Moraine Park

Fern Falls

Odessa Lake

Bear Lake

Glacier Basin

Sprague Lake

Bear Lake Road

ARAPAHO NATIONAL FOREST

Colorado

Kawuneeche Valley

N A T I O N A L

North Inlet Trail

North Inlet

Andrews Glacier

Flattop Mtn 12323

Hallett Peak 12713

Dream Lake

Glacier Gorge Junction

Estes Cone 11007

Lily Lake Visitor Center

Grand Lake Entrance Station

Kawuneeche Visitor Center

Grand Lake

Mt Bryant 11033

Shadow Mountain Lake

East Inlet

Lake Nanita

Taylor Peak 13153

Taylor Glacier

Black Lake

Longs Peak 14255

Glacier Gorge

Storm Pass Trail

Longs Peak

Chiefs Head Peak 13579

Mt Meeker 13911

Chasm Lake

Meeker Park

Pine Beach

Green Ridge

Catthroat Bay

Stillwater

Three Lakes Area

Lake Granby

Mt Alice 13310

Lake Verna

Isolation Peak 13117

Paradise Park

P A R K

Bluebird Lake Trail

Ouzel Falls

Bluebird Lake

Wild Basin

Calypso Cascades

Olive Ridge

Allenspark

Boulder

Granby

Colorado

Twin Peaks 11959

Watanga Mtn 12375

Ogalalla Peak 13136

ROOSEVELT NATIONAL FOREST

Camp Dick

Arapaho Bay

Monarch Lake

Crossing the Continental Divide

Many of the park's highlights can be seen along **Trail Ridge Road**, which runs 48 miles (77km) through the park from east to west following an old Native American trail. This is the highest continuous highway in the country, ranging in elevation from 8,000 to over 12,000 ft (2,438 to 3,658 meters). It crosses the Continental Divide, and you may notice that water on the east side of this mountain backbone runs toward the Atlantic, while streams on the west run toward the Pacific.

This road reveals the grandeur of the Rocky Mountains, with awesome views round every bend. Majestic glacier-carved peaks – 76 of them have elevations of 12,000 ft (3,650 meters) or more – are capped with snow well into summer and form the backdrop for sapphire lakes and verdant valleys. The highest is Longs Peak, which reaches 14,255 ft (3,345 meters). At the higher elevations you can see glaciers and moraines (ridges of rock debris). Lower down, groves of white-barked aspen trees, fluttering with leaves that shine bright yellow in fall, line sparkling streams and hillsides. In summer, mountain meadows are scattered with columbine, Indian paintbrush and some 900 other wildflowers. You may well see mule deer or elk at the side of the road, though you're unlikely to come across the park's more elusive wildlife, including coyote, wild cat, and bear, unless you are hiking in the backcountry.

Driving east to west, the first highlight you'll encounter is **Horseshoe Park**, about 2 miles (3.2km) west of the Falls River entrance station. Here, rangers have set up a bighorn sheep crossing, controling traffic so that the animals can cross from the moraine ridges to the meadow to drink from the salty Sheep Lakes. You'll mainly see them in the mornings in the spring and early summer.

At the upper end of Horseshoe Park is an enormous alluvial fan, where a dam burst in 1982 and sent massive boulders crashing down into the river. Beyond here is the beginning of the **Old Fall River Road**, a narrow, one-way gravel road that leads up through a steep canyon. This was the original road through the park. After 9 miles (14km) it rejoins Trail Ridge Road at the Alpine Visitor Center.

On the main road, you will pass beaver ponds and picnic areas. Soon the towering pine forests give way to sweeping expanses of stark, treeless

Above: rocky terrain

tundra where only tiny alpine flowers and hardy mosses are able to grow. Explore this fragile, windswept world on the Toll Memorial Trail from **Rock Cut**, where a one-hour hiking trail leads through the tundra meadows. It's the only such environment south of the Arctic Circle.

Beyond, you may see huge herds of mule deer grazing in the watery fields to the south. Shortly before you come to the **Alpine Visitor Center** (open 9am–5pm in summer), 6 miles (10 km) farther on, the road reaches its highest point at 12,183ft (3,713 meters). The visitor center sits above the treeline at 11,796ft (3,594 meters. It has interpretive displays, and you can climb higher still up a windy path for spectacular panoramic views of the surrounding tundra, mountains, and snow bowls.

From a Canyon to a Stream

The landscape is gentler on the western side of the park, largely covered with lush forests. You can hike along the **Colorado River Trail** to the ghost town of Lulu City, once a booming mining camp. Here the mighty Colorado, which flows on through seven states and carved out the Grand Canyon, is a mere meandering stream.

To explore the grandest scenery on the east side of the park, take Bear Lake Road, which runs south from the Beaver Meadows entrance station. It leads to the **Moraine Park Museum** (9am–5pm in summer) with exhibits on geology, flora, and fauna. The 9-mile (14km) road twists past looming glaciers and waterfalls to lovely **Bear Lake**, cocooned in a high mountain basin. Along the way are stunning views of Longs Peak. Near the lake is the trailhead for **Glacier Gorge**, one of the best places to see classic glacial features.

A host of outdoor sports such as hiking, rock climbing, and fishing take place within the park and there are several campgrounds. Ranger-led programs and activities are also offered in summer. At either end of the park, both **Estes Park** and **Grand Lake** are pleasant resort towns, with hotels, restaurants, and visitor amenities.

3. BOULDER *(see map, p49)*

There are several attractions in trendy Boulder, but the real joy is soaking up the atmosphere, an activity that repays a longer stay.

Although you can get to Boulder on RTD buses, you'll need a car if you want to visit its outlying attractions. It is a 30-minute drive northwest of Denver on US Highway 36 (known as the Boulder Turnpike), which becomes 28th Street in town. Turn left on Spruce Street to reach the start of the tour at the Hotel Boulderado.

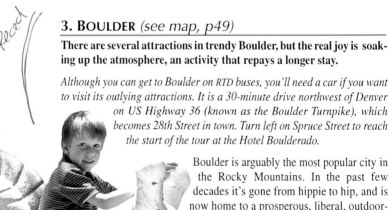

Boulder is arguably the most popular city in the Rocky Mountains. In the past few decades it's gone from hippie to hip, and is now home to a prosperous, liberal, outdoor-sports-crazy population.

As you drive in to Boulder on Highway 36, you will come to the crest of a hill near

Left: having fun on Boulder's Pearl Street Mall

Louisville, beyond which the city spreads out in the valley before you. Its backdrop is the singular peaks of the Flatirons, three red-rock formations with flat faces and jagged ridges jutting into the sky against the foothills of the Rockies. This scenic area was home to a tribe of Arapaho headed by Chief Niwot, until a band of prospectors founded a crude settlement here in 1858 called Boulder City. Their leader, Captain Thomas Aikins, declared that 'the mountains looked right for gold and the valleys looked rich for grazing.' The town became a supply center for more mineral-rich mining camps to the west, and for the farmers on the eastern plains.

Boulder's future path was set when the University of Colorado, known locally as CU, was established here in 1875. Enrolment swelled after World War II, when returning veterans took advantage of the GI Bill which paid for their higher education. Today the university is widely acclaimed and draws professors and students nationwide and from abroad.

In the 1960s and 70s, Boulder ranked with Berkeley, California and other progressive campuses as a hippie haven and hotbed of anti-war protest and environmental activism. Though it has mellowed with age and the changing times, the area remains a mecca for those seeking an alternative lifestyle.

The **Naropa Institute** (2130 Arapahoe Avenue, tel: 303/444-0202), the only Buddhist center of higher education in North America, is located here. Natural food stores, alternative medicine, massage therapists, and New Age

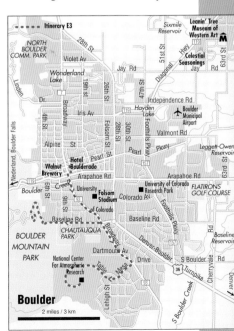

Above: busking in Boulder

bookshops are very much part of the Boulder scene. By and large, its residents are socially conscious, politically liberal, ecology-minded, and concerned with the quality of life. Boulder politicians made early attempts to stem the urban sprawl affecting so many cities along the Front Range by capping growth and buying up land for mountain parks and a greenbelt to surround the town.

Utopia at a Price

There is a laid-back prosperity here as Boulder also attracts many high-tech companies and entrepreneurs. However, Utopia has its price. In recent years the influx of well-heeled newcomers has driven up rents and property prices and increased the demand for services and growth the city has so long sought to avoid. Legend has it that when those first gold-seekers arrived and refused Chief Niwot's request that they go, he put a curse on the city so that anyone who saw it would not want to leave, thus leading to its downfall through overpopulation. Many fear the old Indian's curse may finally be coming true.

Above all, Boulder is in love with the great outdoors. Top athletes come here to train, and it seems this young, physically fit population spends half its time on bicycles, rollerblades or running or hiking along the city's many trails. A favorite is the **Boulder Creek Path**, which runs for 16 miles (26 km) along the waterway that flows through the heart of town. The creek is a second home to kayakers and fly-fishermen, while the Flatirons and nearby mountains attract serious rock climbers and abseilers.

Victorian Landmark

Start your tour at the **Hotel Boulderado**, on the corner of Spruce and 13th streets, a city landmark that opened in 1909. Its name is a conjunction of 'Boulder' and 'Colorado', devised so that guests would always remember where they had stayed. Step into the Victorian lobby to see its beautiful stained-glass ceiling, antique furnishings, and cantilevered cherrywood staircase. The old safe is still in use behind the reception desk, as is the

original Otis elevator. Its rooms are reasonably priced, all things considered. Surprisingly, Boulder was 'dry' until 1967, and no liquor was legally served here until the first bar, the Catacombs, opened in the Boulderado's basement in 1969. It is still a popular watering hole, especially when local blues bands are playing.

From the hotel, walk south on 13th Street for one block to the **Pearl Street Mall**. This four-block pedestrianized stretch of Pearl Street between 11th and 15th streets is the heart and soul of Boulder. Lined with shops, restaurants, art galleries, and sidewalk cafés, it is *the* place for people-watching. It's hopping day and night, and street performers sing, dance, drum, juggle, and provide a stream of quirky, spontaneous entertainment.

Continue south on 13th Street. Turn right on Walnut Street for the **Walnut Street Brewery**, an original Boulder brewpub housed in a century-old brick building. Enormous beer vats line one wall of the spacious interior, and its lively surroundings make a good spot for lunch, dinner (*see page 72*) or simply one of their microbrews.

Further down on 13th Street past Canyon Boulevard is the beautiful **Dushanbe Teahouse** (Mon–Fri 11am–10pm, Sat–Sun 8am–10pm). The teahouse was a gift to the people of Boulder from their sister city, Dushanbe in Tajikistan, to 'make their souls happy.' The exquisite hand-carved plaster panels, columns, tables, and ceiling, decorated with traditional Islamic motifs and painted in vivid colors, were created by 40 Tajik artisans in 1987–90. Four artists came to Boulder to assemble the teahouse, which is the largest outside of Asia. It serves its traditional function as a meeting place, but in addition to a wonderful selection of teas it also serves lunch and dinner (*see page 72*).

Twice a week, an excellent **Farmers' Market** is held alongside and in front of the teahouse. Fresh fruit and vegetables, including organic produce, flowers, honey, baked goods, and other delicious treats are on sale Wednesdays 10am–2pm and Saturdays 8am–2pm, April through October.

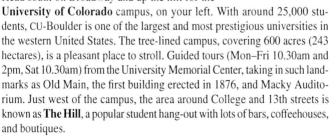

On Campus   Read

The rest of this itinerary is best reached by car. Head south on Broadway and up the hill for the **University of Colorado** campus, on your left. With around 25,000 students, CU-Boulder is one of the largest and most prestigious universities in the western United States. The tree-lined campus, covering 600 acres (243 hectares), is a pleasant place to stroll. Guided tours (Mon–Fri 10.30am and 2pm, Sat 10.30am) from the University Memorial Center, taking in such landmarks as Old Main, the first building erected in 1876, and Macky Auditorium. Just west of the campus, the area around College and 13th streets is known as **The Hill**, a popular student hang-out with lots of bars, coffeehouses, and boutiques.

Top Left: Boulder banner advertising a concert. **Left:** Pearl St Mall, Boulder
Right: decorative details, Boulder Dushanbe Teahouse

Several places of interest lie west of the city. From Broadway, take Baseline Road west to **Chautauqua Park**, located on the 26-acre (10.5-hectare) site at the base of the Flatirons. 'Chautauquas' are summer programs of concerts, plays, and outdoor lectures, a kind of popular education dating back to the 1870s. The historic Dining Hall is open in summer for breakfast, lunch, and dinner, and you can eat outdoors on the porch. The open meadows give fantastic views of the Flatirons, and the park is a gateway to a system of mountain hiking and bicycling trails.

Continue west on Baseline Road which becomes Flagstaff Road. A series of switchbacks leads to the summit of **Flagstaff Mountain** at 6,872 ft (2,095 meters), with hiking trails, picnic spots and fantastic views over Boulder and the Continental Divide.

Natural Forces

South of Baseline Road, take Table Mesa Drive west past more open meadows and grand views to reach the **National Center for Atmospheric Research** (NCAR) (Mon–Fri 8am–5pm, Sat–Sun 9am–4pm). The striking building designed by I M Pei is considered an architectural masterpiece. It was patterned after the ancient cliff dwellings found at Mesa Verde in southwestern Colorado, to harmonize with the Flatirons towering above. Woody Allen's *Sleeper* was filmed at on location here.

NCAR is a national science laboratory, set up to study the complex natural forces that create weather and climate. Although it is not a museum, there are several interactive exhibits in the lobby including an 8-ft (2.5-meter) tall tornado, a fog chamber, and a lightning display. You can take a self-guided tour of this interesting facility, including its super-computer center, and free guided tours are also available (tel: 303/497-

Above: view of the Flatirons from Chautauqua Park
Left: strumming a tune in Boulder

1174 for tour information). There is a short, outdoor trail with interpretive signs that explain different weather conditions.

Also leading west is Canyon Boulevard, which is off Broadway just south of the Pearl Street Mall. It heads up Boulder Canyon (Route 119) to **Nederland**, 16 miles (26km) away, a fun mountain town with a few good bars and restaurants. About halfway up the route you'll see signs for **Boulder Falls** (parking on the left), a 70-ft (21-meter) drop that becomes a cascade during the spring run-off. From Nederland you can head south to Central City (*see Excursion 5, page 57*) or north on Highway 72, the so-called Peak to Peak Highway, to Estes Park and Rocky Mountain National Park (*see Excursion 2, page 45*).

Herbal Highs

Two of Boulder's most interesting attractions lie northeast of the city center. For a quintessentially Boulder multi-sensory experience, take a tour of the **Celestial Seasonings** herbal tea factory. Take the Diagonal Highway (Highway 119) northeast to Jay Road and turn right (east). After 1 mile (1.6km) turn left (north) on Spine Road. After a further half mile (0.8km) turn left (west) onto Sleepytime Drive to the entrance.

Celestial Seasonings, which virtually created the herbal tea industry in America, was the brainchild of a visionary hippie businessman who took flower power to its limits. In 1969, 19-year-old Mo Siegel and friends gathered wild herbs in the Rocky Mountains and began blending them into teas which they packaged and sold to health-food stores. Working from an old barn on the edge of town, they expanded the business and began importing herbs to create new flavors. Red Zinger, introduced in 1972, was an immediate hit and sold nationwide. Today Celestial Seasonings is the largest herbal tea manufacturer in the country, with more than 60 varieties of herb and black teas.

The free, 45-minute tour (given on the hour Mon–Sat 10am–3pm and Sun 11am–3pm, on a first-come, first-served basis). begins in the art gallery, which features the original paintings used on the colorful tea packages, and an eclectic teapot collection. You then enter the factory, where you're greeted with heavenly aromas emanating from towering pallets of herbs from around the world. Step into the mint room for an eye-watering blast to the senses. The automated production line is fascinating, filling and packaging 2 million tea bags per day (it's best to come on a weekday when the production line is in operation). You can sample the teas, stroll in the herb garden, and browse in the tea shop.

The Celestial Cafe, open for breakfast (7.30–9.30am) and lunch (11am–2.30pm), serves good food, including vegetarian dishes.

Two blocks north on Longbow Drive is the **Leanin' Tree Museum of Western Art** (Mon–Fri 8am–4.30pm and Sat–Sun 10am–4pm). Assembled

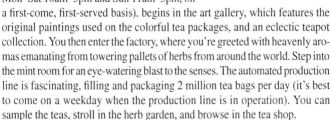

Right: tea-tasting at the Celestial Seasonings tour center

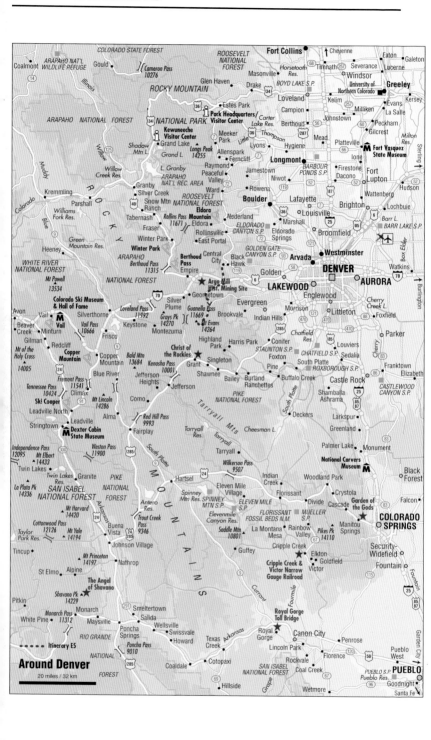

Around Denver

20 miles / 32 km

by Ed Trumble, who started collecting in the 1950s as he searched for artwork for his greeting cards company, it has grown into one of the largest private collections of Western art in the nation. It contains nearly 300 paintings and 85 bronzes depicting cowboys, Native Americans, landscapes, wildlife, and scenes from frontier and ranch life. Western art is a unique American genre, derived from popular expression and not recognized by mainstream scholars. This fascinating collection features work by over 90 artists, including portraits by Bill Hampton (1925–77), panoramic landscapes by Bill Hughes (1932–93), and humorous scenes of old cow camps by Jack Roberts (1920–2000).

For an alternative route back to Denver, turn left as you leave the museum and then left again on North 63rd Street. Turn right on Highway 119 and right again on Highway 52 which intersects with I-25 south to Denver.

4. WINTER PARK *(see map p54)*

Denver has its own ski resort, Winter Park. With exciting terrain and trails on two mountains, it is the fourth largest ski area in the Rockies, and one of the most popular. Hiking, bicycling and a fantastic Alpine Slide make this a great summer getaway, too.

Winter Park is 67 miles (108km) from Denver, about 1½ hours' drive. Take I-70 West to Empire and exit onto US 40, which climbs over Berthoud Pass to Winter Park. On weekends you can also take the Ski Train from Denver's Union Station.

Winter Park, owned by the City of Denver, is one of its most popular mountain parks. Set high in the Arapaho National Forest, the vast stretch of surrounding public land affords unspoiled views of the mountain peaks, many of them topping 13,000 feet (3,962 meters). Though it was developed as a ski resort in the 1940s, people have been coming here to ski since 1927. That year, the Moffat Railroad Tunnel was completed, bringing skiers to the Fraser Valley, where they would hike uphill for a run down the mountain on 7-ft (2-meter) long wooden skis.

Today the resort is an international ski destination with 121 trails and 20 lifts spread between Winter Park and its sister mountain, Mary Jane. Its variety of terrain and proximity to Denver make it one of the most popular ski areas in Colorado. There is one thing Winter Park lacks – snobbery. People come here to have a good time, not to see and be seen.

The town of Winter Park, 5 miles (8 km) past the resort at the base of the mountain, spreads into the valley. There are stores, hotels, amenities, and good restaurants (*see page 72*). The pace here is laid back and friendly. Farther down the valley, the town of Fraser has the dubious dis-

Right: mountain bike chair lift in summer

tinction of being the 'icebox of the nation,' as winter temperatures here are often the coldest on the weather map. The Amtrak train stops here on its way to California.

Winter Park is also a wonderful place to visit in summer. The resort has a host of activities for families, including the Human Maze, outdoor Climbing Wall, mini-golf, Zip Line cable ride and the Skybounce, where you can bounce up to 100 ft (30.5 meters) high tethered to a huge helium balloon. Or just relax and soak up the mountain scenery and fresh air, with a stroll through forests and alpine meadows.

Riding High

Don't miss the **Alpine Slide**, the longest in Colorado, which twists through 26 linked turns as it whisks you over 3,000ft (923 meters) down the mountain. Ride the slide on a plastic sled with hand-controled brakes at a speed comfortable for you. There are two tracks, so you can choose the fast lane or the slow one. This is tremendous fun, for adults as much as for kids, and though you can buy tickets for single rides, buy a half-day pass as you'll probably want at least one more ride. Take the Arrow chairlift to the top.

Nearby, the **Zephyr Express** chairlift takes you to the summit of Winter Park mountain, 10,700ft (3,261 meters) high. It's a stunning ride, with magnificent vistas of the forest and the surrounding mountain peaks. Have a drink or a bite to eat at **The Lodge at Sunspot** (11am–3pm), which serves grilled sandwiches, salads, chili, and bakery treats. You can ride back down, or set off to explore hiking trails of varying difficulty. The Ute Trail is a self-guided nature hike back down below the lift, while the Nystrom Trail climbs up to the Parsenn Bowl, elevation 12,060ft (3,676 meters).

Winter Park is a favorite spot for mountain bikers, too, with over 50 miles (80 km) of trails accessible by chairlift and rated like ski trails that connect

with a 600-mile (966-km) trail system. The resort has a bicycle shop with rentals and repairs, and maintains a bicycle patrol on the mountain.

Special events take place throughout the summer, including the Winter Park Jazz Festival and the World Class RockFest, both held in July; the Rocky Mountain Wine, Beer, and Food Festival in August, and the Oktoberfest celebration in late September/early October. The resort is open in summer 10am–6pm and in September on weekends only, 10am–5pm, weather permitting. You can pay for single activities or buy a multiple activity pass.

The **Ski Train** (Fri–Sun, Dec–Apr and on Sat in summer from mid-June to mid-Aug, leaving downtown Denver at 8am and leaving Winter Park at 3.30pm) from Denver's Union Station to the base of the lifts at Winter Park is an enjoyable way to reach the resort. On the two-hour journey into the mountains the train burrows through 34 tunnels and traverses narrow ledges high above rivers and forests.

5. CENTRAL CITY *(see map p54)*

During its heyday as a gold mining town in the 1860s, Central City was known as the 'richest square mile on Earth,' so seek your fortune at a casino in one of the town's Victorian buildings. Everything can be easily explored in an hour, but you may end up gambling the night away. Return to Denver on the highest paved road in North America.

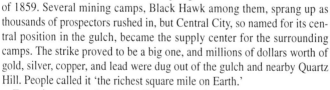

Central City and neighboring Black Hawk are 34 miles (55km) west of Denver. From I-70 take the Highway 6 exit, veering off onto Highway 119 as signposted. The drive takes about 45 minutes. Bus transportation can also be arranged through many casinos or the Opera House.

This area was the scene of Colorado's first major gold rush, which began when gold was discovered in Gregory Gulch in the spring of 1859. Several mining camps, Black Hawk among them, sprang up as thousands of prospectors rushed in, but Central City, so named for its central position in the gulch, became the supply center for the surrounding camps. The strike proved to be a big one, and millions of dollars worth of gold, silver, copper, and lead were dug out of the gulch and nearby Quartz Hill. People called it 'the richest square mile on Earth.'

For a time during the 1860s, Central City rivaled Denver as the largest town in the Colorado territory. Cornish miners from England made their mark by introducing buildings with mortarless stone walls, many of which still stand. The prosperous residents loved theater and opera, and in 1878 the new Opera House opened to great acclaim, even drawing patrons from Denver. But by the turn of the century, the gold fields were petering out along with Central City's fortunes. Although the Opera House reopened in 1932 after a four-year closure, historic tourism failed to bring enough revenue to the town.

Top Left: Alpine Slide, Winter Park. **Left:** skiing in Winter Park
Right: Central City Opera House

Then, in 1990, the wheel of fortune spun again and Colorado voters legalized gambling in Central City, Black Hawk, and Cripple Creek. Central City's historic buildings now house casinos, and the streets ring with the sounds of slot machines, clattering coins, and busloads of tourists coming up for a flutter. With a $5 betting limit, it's hardly Las Vegas. Nonetheless, the roads into town can see bumper-to-bumper traffic on busy gambling nights.

Critics say the gambling has spoiled the town's historic character. It certainly raised property prices, causing many long-time residents to sell up and leave. Central City and Black Hawk aren't to everyone's taste, but it has to be said that the casinos have given these once-dying towns a new lease on life.

Black Hawk to Central City

The drive up through the canyon is a pretty one, alongside the mountain stream where eager prospectors once panned for gold. Any charm Black Hawk might once have had has been swallowed up by the monstrous purpose-built casino and parking structure hulking on the edge of town. Apart from the **Lace House** (161 Main Street, daily 10am–4pm in summer; admission fee), a gingerbread-like house built in Carpenter Gothic style, hurry past to Central City, where the atmosphere and fine Victorian facades which line Main and Eureka streets, are more rewarding.

The main attraction is the historic **Central City Opera House** (tel: 303/292-6700 or 800/851-8175) at the top of Eureka Street, which presents three operas during the summer season in this intimate 550-seat theater. Sarah Bernhardt, Edwin Booth, and Lillian Gish, as well as other leading stars performed here. The Opera House is open for performances only and the season runs from the end of June through early August.

Next door is the **Teller House**, Central City's premier hotel when it was built in 1872. Luminaries from President Ulysses S. Grant to Mae West stayed in these luxurious rooms. For the commoner, its downstairs bar is more famous as the home of the 'Face on the Barroom Floor,' that of a mysteri-

Above: Teller House, Central City

ous woman painted by Herndon Davis in 1936. Today the hotel houses a casino and restaurant. William's Stables, opposite, makes an atmospheric venue for afternoon cabaret opera performances.

The town's two museums are open only in summer. These include the **Gilpin County Historical Society Museum** (228 East High Street; daily 11am–4pm, admission fee) with displays on life in the old mining towns, and the **Thomas-Billings House** (209 Eureka Street, 11am–4pm; admission fee) where you can see what life was like in an 1874 Victorian family home. It's also fun to explore the historic cemeteries and nearby ghost towns such as **Nevadaville**, reached by heading west on Eureka Street past the opera house.

For a breathtaking alternative route out of town, take Spring Street south past the train station, which leads onto the aptly named **Oh My God Road**. The narrow path up Virginia Canyon has some steep drop-offs and passes the remnants of old mine shafts and camps on the way to Idaho Springs, 9 miles (14km) away, where you can catch I-70 back to Denver.

For more scenic views, however, from Idaho Springs take Highway 103 south to Echo Lake, where the road to the top of **Mount Evans** begins (summer only; admission fee). This scenic byway climbs 14 miles (22.5 km) to the 14,264-ft (4,348-meter) summit along the highest paved road in North America. From here there is a fantastic view of the entire Front Range and the Continental Divide. You may see a mountain goat near the top, as a large herd is sheltered here. You can also walk the Mount Goliath Nature Trail, where the 2,000-year-old bristle-cone pine trees are among the oldest living things on earth.

6. GEORGETOWN *(see map p60)*

Once known as the Silver Queen of the Rockies, Georgetown is one of Colorado's finest historic towns. Stroll through the streets lined with restored Victorian homes and buildings, take a ride on the delightful Georgetown Loop narrow-gauge railroad, and visit a silver mine.

Book tickets on the Georgetown Loop, tel: 303/569-2403, and enquire about visiting the Lebanese Silver Mine en route. Bring sunscreen, a hat, and a sweater. Georgetown is 50 miles (80 km) west of Denver via I-70. The drive takes about an hour, but allow extra time for traffic delays.

Georgetown lies in a scenic valley surrounded by 12,000-ft (3,658-meter) mountains. It was founded when two brothers, George and David Griffith, struck gold in Upper Clear Creek Canyon in 1859 and named their mining camp after the elder brother. By the mid-1860s, however, rich veins of silver in the surrounding mountains yielded an even bigger bonanza for Georgetown. The 'Silver Queen of the Rockies,' as it was known in its heyday,

Right: Georgetown

produced more silver than any other mining area in the world until surpassed by the Leadville strike in 1878. Some estimate that as much as $200 million worth of silver was extracted here.

The town thrived and at one point in the 1870s it was the third largest in the state with more than 5,000 residents, who built many beautiful family homes in a variety of architectural styles. While most towns of that era succumbed to devastating fires, Georgetown's volunteer fire department kept a vigilant watch over the town, allowing more than 200 original buildings to survive to the present day. The old firehouse with its tall tower, Alpine Hose No 2, dates from 1874 and stands on 5th Street.

Today Georgetown is a **National Historic District** and beautifully restored buildings fill the town center. A local preservation group helps residents to maintain their homes in accurate period style, right down to the color of the paint. Handsome commercial buildings on 6th Street now house restaurants and interesting stores, including one selling home-made ice cream. You can see the Downtown district on foot, or take a horse-drawn buggy.

Toward the end of 6th Street is the **Hotel de Paris** (late May–early Sept: daily 11am–4.30pm; rest of Sept: Fri–Mon 12 noon–4pm, Oct–May: Sat–Sun 12 noon–4pm; admission fee). This was built in 1875 by a Frenchman, Louis Dupuy, who wanted to preserve the spirit of his home country. The hotel was one of the finest in the West, with carved walnut furniture, Haviland china, lace curtains, and other luxurious furnishings, including steam heat and hot running water. Louis himself was a scholar, philosopher, and master chef, and the hotel became famous throughout the country for its cuisine, fine wines, and good company. The restored building, filled with its original furnishings, is now a museum.

Another of Georgetown's outstanding buildings is the **Hamill House Museum** (June–Sept: daily 10am–5pm; Oct–Dec: weekends 12 noon–4pm; admission fee). This country-style Gothic Revival house was built in 1867, but enlarged in 1879 by its new owner, Arthur Hamill,

Above: Hamill House Museum
Right: Georgetown Loop railroad

who had made his fortune in silver. Its elegant interior contains many original furnishings.

Through Devil's Gate by Steam Train

The highlight of Georgetown, however, is the **Georgetown Loop Railway** (daily end-May–Sept; admission charge). This authentic, narrow-gauge steam train ran between Georgetown and the neighboring mining town of Silver Plume. Although it lies just 2 miles (3.2 km) up the valley, the difference in elevation is over 600ft (183 meters). The rail track winds through the mountains to gain this elevation, and traverses the dramatic **Devil's Gate Viaduct**, a trestle 300ft (90 meters) long and 100ft (30 meters) high that forms a spiral where the track crosses over itself.

The round-trip ride takes an hour and 10 minutes. Many of the cars are open topped, so bring a hat and sunscreen. The train stops briefly near the **Lebanon Silver Mine**, where you can take an optional tour (1 hour 20 minutes) for an additional charge; bring a sweater as the temperature below ground is a constant 44°F (7°C).

You can catch the train at either the Devil's Gate boarding area in Georgetown or at the Silver Plume boarding area. It's wise to book ahead for this popular trip (tel: 303/569-2403). Departure times are every hour and 20 minutes from 10am (Devil's Gate) and from 9.20am (Silver Plume).

The little town of **Silver Plume** is also worth a detour. Its one street is lined with weathered false-front buildings. Stop into the Sopp & Truscott bakery at the far end for delicious homemade preserves and other treats.

Before You Go

Back in Georgetown, drive along Georgetown Lake to the **Watchable Wildlife Viewing Station** to see if you can spot any Rocky Mountain Bighorn Sheep on the mountainsides. At the other end of town is the start of the **Guanella Pass Scenic Byway**, a 22-mile (35km) route that passes historic sites on its way to the 11,669-ft (3,557-meter) summit. From there the road drops down to the town of Grant, where you can catch Highway 285 back to Denver.

7. VAIL AND VICINITY *(see map p54)*

Vail is the trendy mountain spot for a weekend getaway from Denver. It is nearly as popular in summer as during the ski season.

Book accommodation from the Vail Valley Tourism and Convention Bureau, tel: 800/525-3875, or online at www.visitvailvalley.com. *Vail is located about 110 miles (176km) west of Denver via I-70. The drive takes about 2 hours, but allow more time in winter to negotiate Vail Pass.*

In contrast to its more rustic mountain neighbors, Vail is a sleek, modern resort built to resemble an Alpine village, complete with horse-drawn carriage rides. It sits at 8,250ft (2,515 meters) above sea level and though the

valley now contains some of the most expensive real estate in the Rockies, it was an isolated backwater until 1962, when Pete Seibert established the ski area after training here as a mountain paratrooper during World War II. Today Vail is the largest single ski complex in North America, with three base areas and some 4,700 acres (1,900 hectares) of skiing terrain, including the famous powder-filled back bowls. Hundreds of upscale apartment blocks, shops and restaurants spread along the narrow valley, and the resort attracts a sophisticated, international clientele.

Village Views

A free public bus runs between East and West Vail, linking the two pedestrianized villages – **Vail** and **Lionshead** – at the base of the ski lifts. Two chairlifts operate in summer, giving access to miles of mountain trails for hiking and bicycling. The Eagle Bahn Gondola from Lionshead affords panoramic views as it carries you more than 2,000ft (610 meters) up to **Eagle's Nest**. There are vistas of the Sawatch range and the Mount of the Holy Cross to the south and the jagged Gore Range to the north. You can have lunch here, rent mountain bikes, play horseshoes, or disc golf or try other activities at the **Adventure Ridge** playground. Trails of varying difficulty lead higher still into the mountains, or across the slopes to the Vista Bahn Express chairlift, which will take you down to Vail Village. In town, other diversions include the **Colorado Ski Museum**, the Vail Nature Center, and the Betty Ford Alpine Gardens (open daily until snowfall).

A few miles west is the newer, more exclusive resort of **Beaver Creek**, which opened in 1980. It is known for its advanced-level ski runs, but, like Vail, has a summer program of activities on the mountain.

Another big attraction of this area is the large number of summer festivals and events. Two highlights are the Vail International Dance Festival and the Vail Jazz Festival, held in July and August. And, if you're around for the Fourth of July, the town of **Avon**, at the base of Beaver Creek, puts on the biggest and the best fireworks show in Colorado.

Above: guided hike on Vail Mountain
Right: on the slopes

Leisure
Activities

SHOPPING

Denver is wonderful for shopping, from the art galleries of LoDo to the sleek malls at Cherry Creek and Park Meadows. With the demise of the Downtown department stores in the 1970s and '80s and the rise of suburban malls, shopping areas can be found all around the metro area. Denver has more sporting goods stores per capita than anywhere else, and it is also home to one of the largest independent book stores in the nation, the Tattered Cover.

Opening hours are generally 9am until 5 or 6pm, and some Downtown or local stores may be closed all day on Sundays. Shopping malls are open daily until 9 or 10pm. Many convenience stores are open 24 hours. Note that all liquor stores in Colorado are closed on Sunday.

Shopping in Denver entails a 7½ percent sales tax, which is added to the sticker price at the check-out.

Sporting Goods

Some of the best buys in Denver are sporting goods. Both outdoor clothing and sports gear, from skis to backpacks, are less expensive here than in the mountain resorts, and the range of brands and styles is extensive. **Gart Brothers Sports Castle** at 10th Street and Broadway is said to be the largest sporting goods store in the world, with entire floors dedicated to a single sport, such as skiing. There are 17 other metro locations.

Hot on its heels is the enormous **REI** store at 15th and Platte streets, beside Confluence Park, with a rock-climbing wall and a cold room for testing arctic weather apparel. Other Downtown stores include **Great Pacific Patagonia** (15th Street) with a line of Patagonia clothing; **Eastern Mountain Sports** (1616 Welton and other metro locations) and **Grand West Outfitters** (801 Broadway). Keen runners should check out **Nike Town** (16th Street Mall) and **Runner's Roost** (1001

16th Street). **Colorado Ski & Golf** (2680 South Havana in Aurora) offers low prices on top-brand equipment.

Western Goods

It is increasingly hard to find a cowboy hat in cosmopolitan Denver, but the place to get fitted out in authentic cowboy boots and clothing is **Miller Stockman Western Wear** on California Street – it has been in business since 1918. **Made in Colorado** (4840 W. 29th Avenue) is a store selling everything from gold panning kits to jewelry and gourmet foods – as long as it is produced in the state. **Cry Baby Ranch** on Larimer Street has all kinds of cowboy kitsch and Western furnishings, while the **Denver Buffalo Company** on Lincoln Avenue has an instore teepee, a trading post, cowboy souvenirs, Western art, and foodstuffs.

Native American Crafts

Denver is a good place to look for Native American crafts. The **Mudhead Gallery**, located in both the Brown Palace and Hyatt Regency hotels downtown, has top-quality sculptures and Southwestern art. The **Native American Trading Company** on Bannock Street sells high-quality textiles, jewelry, paintings, and pottery.

West Southwest on Fillmore Street has jewelry, artworks, pottery, and gifts. Beautiful Mexican pottery and crafts can be found at **Manos Folk Art** (101 Broadway), **Old Santa Fe Pottery** (2485 South Santa Fe

Left: sale of psychedelia, Civic Center Park
Right: Foss General Store sign, Golden

Drive) and **Galeria Mexicana** (3615 West 32nd Avenue), which sells imported goods from villages south of the border.

Downtown

Along the 16th Street Mall is an eclectic mix of stores. In between the cafés and coffee shops you'll find books, shoes, candles, cameras, wigs, and pharmacies, along with tourist stores selling T-shirts and souvenirs. The huge **Media Play**, with books, magazines, music, and computer software, now

occupies the old Denver Dry Goods department store along with **T J Maxx**.

The biggest addition to Downtown is the **Denver Pavilions**, a flashy complex of stores, restaurants, and movie theaters that straddles two square blocks, linked by a neon marquee. Denver's favorite megastores are here – **Virgin Records**, **Nike Town**, and **Barnes & Noble** – along with clothing stores such as Banana Republic, Ann Taylor, and Gap, Victoria's Secret lingerie, and stores specializing in bath products, luggage, sunglasses, and chocolates. You'll also find mega-restaurants, in terms of size and quality, including Wolfgang Puck Cafe, Café Odyssey, Maggiano's Little Italy, and the Hard Rock Cafe.

Farther along between Arapahoe and Lawrence is the **Tabor Center**, a glass-walled complex of small clothing stores and specialty stores selling cigars, kites, and flags. Nearby, the renovated buildings of **Writer Square** also house small, interesting stores.

The handsome Victorian brick buildings of **Larimer Square**, Denver's oldest street, now house a fine collection of art galleries, restaurants and nightclubs, and high-quality stores. Look for **John Atencio** or **Gusterman Silversmiths** (jewelry), the **Z Gallerie** (home furnishings and accessories), and **Earthzone**, a mineral and fossil gallery.

Throughout **LoDo** there are stores and art galleries showcasing contemporary, traditional, and ethnic arts and crafts, from paintings to furniture. Two favorites are **Wazee Deco Antiques** (1730 Wazee Street) and **The Baobab Tree** (1518 Wazee) selling African crafts. The Lower Downtown Arts District stretches between 14th and 25th streets from Larimer to Wazee. The First Friday Art Walk, conducted from 5–9pm on the first Friday of each month, offers the chance to visit over 25 galleries in Denver's biggest arts district (tel: 303/820-3139; www.denvergalleries.com). The **Pacific Mercantile Company** (1925 Lawrence) at Sakura Square has an amazing array of Asian foods and ingredients, as well as gift items.

Cherry Creek

The **Cherry Creek Shopping Center** opened in 1990 as Colorado's premier shopping mall and was Denver's first upscale shopping area. Between its four anchor department stores – Neiman Marcus, Lord & Taylor, Saks Fifth Avenue, and Foleys – it has top-quality goods and fine fashions in stores that attract shoppers from around the world. These include Tiffany, Louis Vuitton, FAO Schwarz, Eddie Bauer, and Williams Sonoma, as well as the delightful Build-a-Bear Workshop where you can construct your own teddy bear.

Opposite the mall, **Cherry Creek North** comprises 16 blocks of art galleries, boutiques, cafes, and restaurants. It is home to the famous **Tattered Cover Book Store** (1st Avenue at Milwaukee), with four floors of books, magazines, and reading nooks. There is another branch in LoDo.

Suburban Malls

There are shopping malls in all of Denver's major suburbs, including the **Aurora Mall** and **Southglenn Mall** in Littleton. But two

Above: Denver Pavilions, Downtown. **Top Right**: Cherry Creek Shopping Center
Right: Highway 74, the main road through Evergreen

If you're after bargains, **Castle Rock Factory Outlets**, about 20 miles (32km) south of Denver on I-25, is one of the largest malls of its kind, with over 130 outlet stores. You can pick up top brand names and designer fashions for much less than the standard retail price. Quality varies, however, and you can often find equally good bargains during sales at department stores in town.

One-of-a-Kind Shops

Two delightful neighborhood shopping streets near Washington Park offer a respite from the malls. **South Gaylord Street**, between Mississippi and Tennessee avenues, is an historic district of charming restaurants and stores, such as the **Art Pedlar** pottery shop and **Trout's**, which sells fishing gear and clothing. **South Pearl Street**, between Louisiana and Iowa avenues, has more one-of-a-kind stores and restaurants, including the **Denver Doll Emporium**, **Murder by the Book** mystery bookstore, and shops selling quilts and antiques.

Boulder

Boulder is the best place to indulge in alternative culture. Here you'll find plenty of New Age booktores, health food stores, and music stores, on and around the **Pearl Street Mall**. **Alfalfa's Market** (1651 Broadway, Boulder) has a great range of natural soaps, shampoos, and body-care products as well as natural foods.

The Lighthouse, at Pearl Street and Broadway, has a vast range of books on all manner of metaphysical subjects.

of them rival Cherry Creek as shopping attractions. Hailed as a retail 'resort', **Park Meadows** opened in Littleton in 1996 with Nordstrom, Dillard's, and the largest Foley's department store in the state as its anchors. It was designed to look like a ski lodge, with a huge center court fireplace. Its 130 stores and restaurants suit all budgets, though the fact that they are grouped into 'districts' (the Lifestyle District, Fashion District, and so forth) makes you feel like you're in a shopping theme park. At the perimeter of the mall is **Nordstrom Rack**, which sells cut-price Nordstrom clothing and other goods.

Flatiron Crossing opened in 2000 on US 36 between Denver and Boulder, with Nordstrom, Dillard's, Lord & Taylor, and a range of other stores and restaurants.

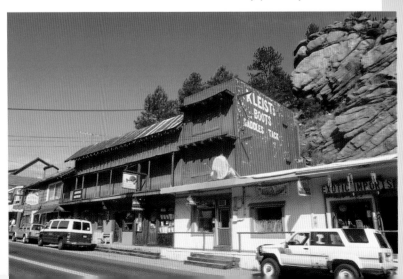

EATING OUT

Dining in Denver is a lot of fun. Both Downtown and throughout the metro area, there are plenty of lively and attractive places for casual meals, as well as sophisticated restaurants for intimate, formal dining. Many of Colorado's brewpubs serve excellent pub fare and light meals. Cafés are also popular.

One of Denver's last links to its cow-town origins is its palate. Here, you can not only see a buffalo, you can eat one. Buffalo is raised commercially in Colorado and is served in many restaurants as steaks, burgers, and even hot dogs. Venison, elk, and other game dishes are also popular. Beef is still king, however, and Denver has excellent steakhouses, while steak and burgers are found on most menus.

There is no lack of fresh seafood in landlocked Denver – it's flown in daily from the coast. Fresh fish features on many menus, including Rocky Mountain rainbow trout, a local favorite. Most restaurants have vegetarian dishes; try the giant portobello mushrooms, delicious when grilled, with a consistency reminiscent of tender steak.

World cuisine is popular in Denver, and you can find just about any type of ethnic dish you desire, from Mexican and Southwestern specialties to Brazilian grills to inventive Thai and Asian cuisine. Many restaurants mix it up, with a variety of entrees that reflect an innovative global flair.

Most Denver restaurants are informal, though you may want to dress up for the more sophisticated establishments. Reservations are advised for popular, upscale restaurants.

Price Guide

Based on the cost of a three-course meal for one, excluding drinks and tip
$ – Inexpensive (under $15)
$$ – Moderate ($15–30)
$$$ – Expensive (over $30)

Denver
Colorado Cuisine

Buckhorn Exchange
1000 Osage Street
Tel: 303/534-9505
Denver's oldest restaurant, serving buffalo steaks and elk in an Old-West setting. $$$

The Denver Buffalo Company

1109 Lincoln Street
Tel: 303/832-0880
Informal family dining in this Western-themed restaurant, trading post, and deli, which specializes in buffalo, beef, elk, and other frontier-style fare. $$

The Fort

19192 Route 8, off West Hampden near Morrison
Tel: 303/697-4771
Denverites love this restaurant, set in a re-created adobe fur-trading post, which serves

Above: Morton's of Chicago steakhouse in LoDo

food and drink of the early American West. Start with a Hailstorm (Colorado's first mixed drink, a prickly pear Margarita), rattlesnake cakes, or bison marrow bones, followed by a buffalo steak, elk medallions, or charbroiled quail. The adobe bricks were made on site, and hand-hewn beams and fireplaces complete the Western atmosphere. Attentive service and fabulous mountain views. $$$

American
The Broker
821 17th Street
Tel: 303/292-5065
Romantic dining in a genuine bank vault. Fine steaks and seafood. $$$

The Cheesecake Factory
Tabor Center, 16th and Larimer streets
Tel: 303/595-0333
You may be drawn in by 34 kinds of cheesecake and patio dining along the 16th Street Mall, but take a look at the extensive menu, from pasta to steaks and seafood. Dinner served late. Take-out available. $$

The Ship Tavern
Brown Palace Hotel, 321 17th Street
Tel: 303/297-3111
Prime rib is the signature dish at this atmospheric restaurant, where other choices range from buffalo burgers to Rocky Mountain trout. Antique models of schooners and clipper ships adorn the walls, while Jamaican rum barrels and an authentic mast and crow's nest complete the nautical theme in the hotel's oldest dining spot. The piano bar Tuesday–Saturday nights is the best in town. $$

Steakhouses
Morton's of Chicago
1710 Wynkoop
Tel: 303/825-3353
Steaks don't come any finer than Morton's USDA prime aged beef. Many of the restaurants's waiters are resting actors who give a theatrical presentation of the day's choices (which include seafood). Excellent wine and martini list. Classy decor with dark wood paneling, leather booths, and celebrity photos on the walls. Buzzy atmosphere in the heart of LoDo. $$$

Rodizio Grill
1801 Wynkoop
Tel: 303/294-9277
Eat as much as you like at this Brazilian steakhouse, where over a dozen grilled meats are rotated to your table. Fantastic salad bar. $$

Seafood
McCormick's Fish House & Bar
1659 Wazee
Tel: 303/825-1107
Denver's premier seafood spot, with more than 30 varieties of fresh fish and seafood, as well as prime meats and pasta. $$$

Continental
Ellyngton's
Brown Palace Hotel, 321 17th Street
Tel: 303/297-3111
Many a power deal is clinched over the excellent food here. Fantastic jazz and champagne brunch on Sundays. $$

The Palace Arms
Brown Palace Hotel, 321 17th Street
Tel: 303/297-3111
Award-winning cuisine in a class restaurant decorated to reflect the Napoleonic period. Contains 17th-century antiques. $$$

Papillon Cafe
250 Josephine Street, Cherry Creek North.
Tel: 303/333-7166
Romantic, highly acclaimed restaurant serving French Continental cuisine with a Thai influence. $$$

Contemporary
California Pizza Kitchen
Cherry Creek Shopping Center
Tel: 303/388-5686
Popular spot for inventive pizzas, as well as pasta, salads, and sandwiches. $

Cafe Odyssey
500 16th Street, 3rd level at Denver Pavilions
Tel: 303/260-6100
Where in the world will you eat today? This enjoyable restaurant has themed rooms, from Africa to Atlantis, and an international menu to match. House favorites include *fajitas*, risotto, steaks, and jambalaya, along with a range of salads, pasta, and pizza. $$

Restaurant Kevin Taylor
1106 14th Street, Hotel Teatro
Tel: 303/820-2600
Outstanding American contemporary cuisine from a nationally acclaimed chef, served in an elegant dining room. $$$

Roy's
3000 East 1st Avenue,
Cherry Creek Shopping Center
Tel: 303/333-9300
Creative Polynesian and Asian fusion cuisine, with delectable fish dishes and surprises like Yama Mama meatloaf. $$$

Sacré Bleu
410 East 7th Avenue
Tel: 303/832-6614
Sacré Bleu offers intimate dining in sensuous surroundings; a hot place to 'see and be seen.' Try the black truffle souffle. Good wine list. $$$

Sambuca
1320 15th Street
Tel: 303/629-5299
Come here fore good fresh fish, grilled beef, fresh pasta, plus a side order of live jazz, which is staged nightly at this trendy LoDo restaurant. $$

Vesta Dipping Grill
1822 Blake Street
Tel: 303/296-1970
This is a fashionable LoDo hot-spot for good ethnic cuisine, in particular dipping 'world grill' food into a selection of exotic sauces. $$

Wolfgang Puck Cafe
500 16th Street, 2nd level, Denver Pavilions
Tel: 303/595-9653
Denverites can 'live, love, eat' now that this beloved California chef has opened one of his stylish grand cafés on the 16th Street Mall. The imaginative cuisine has a Pacific Rim influence, from sushi to satay dishes and stir-fried Pad Thai. The fire-roasted portobello mushrooms are exquisite. Steaks, chicken, seafood, pasta, sandwiches, salads, and Wolf's famous wood-fired pizzas are all cooked with flair. Save room for the Bullseye cheesecake and key lime pie. $$

Italian
Josephina's Ristorante
1433 Larimer Street
Tel: 303/623-0166
A Larimer Square institution, serving New Age pastas, chicken, veal, and seafood. Live music nightly. $$

Maggiano's Little Italy
500 16th Street, Denver Pavilions
Tel: 303/260-7707
Generous portions of delicious Southern Italian cuisine are served in this large, comfortable restaurant, with dark wood and red-checked tablecloths. Mushroom ravioli, baked shrimp and *calamari* are among the appetizers. Excellent choice of pasta, seafood, chicken, vea, and steaks, accompanied by a great wine list. Half orders of pasta and family-style dinners are available. $$

Panzano
909 17th Street
Tel: 303/296-3525
Situated adjacent to the Hotel Monaco, this Downtown restaurant serves outstanding Northern Italian cuisine in an intimate setting, with dark paneling, private booths, and hand-painted murals on the ceiling. Start with grilled black mission figs wrapped in parma ham, or pancetta wrapped shrimp. The rack of lamb and veal medallions are superb. Boutique Italian wines add flavor to the food. Save room for the fantastic desserts. $$$

Mexican and Southwestern
Canyon Cafe
2500 East 1st Avenue,
Cherry Creek Shopping Center
Tel: 303/321-2700
Specialises in creative Southwestern dishes ranging from wild boar *quesadillas* to venison *pasole*. Also well-known for its great Margaritas. $$

Chipotle Mexican Grill
140 Steele Street
Tel: 303/329-6466
Chipotle has been voted Denver's best place for burrito – and other take-out Mexican fare. Outlets can be found throughout the metropolitan area. $

Señoritas Cantina

1700 Wynkoop
Tel: 303/298-7181

Señoritas Cantina is LoDo's most popular Mexican hot spot, serving delicious mesquite-grilled *fajitas*, quail, and seafood *enchiladas* along with a range of traditional Mexican fare. $$

Chinese

P F Chang's

1415 15th Street
Tel: 303/260-7222

First-rate culinary creations from all the major regions of China. The contemporary Chinese bistro setting suits its trendy LoDo location. $$

Bars and Cafés

The Cherry Cricket

2641 E Second Avenue
Tel: 303/322-7666

This Cherry Creek hole-in-the-wall is a firm favorite with Denverites on account of its wonderful burgers and powerful green chiles. $

My Brother's Bar

2376 15th Street
Tel: 303/455-9991

My Brother's Bar is a long-loved Denver watering hole. It is also a top contender for serving the best burgers in town, and offers live classical music on Saturday nights. Closed Sunday. $

Rock Bottom Brewery

1001 16th Street
Tel: 303/534-7616

Serves great brews and good grub, from tasty sandwiches or a plate of pasta to lunch and dinner entrees. It also offers a large patio on the Mall, which is perfect for people-watching. $–$$

Wynkoop Brewing Company

1634 18th Street
Tel: 303/297-2700

Denver's original brewpub, Wynkoop Brweing Company offers its loyal customers good pub fare, sandwiches, and delicious lunch and dinner entrees – along with very good beer. $–$$

Boulder

Q's Restaurant

2115 13th Street
Tel: 303/442-4880

This sleek restaurant located in the Hotel Boulderado is one of Colorado's finest dining establishment. The contemporary American menu changes seasonally to serve the freshest selections of seafood, meat, game, and vegetarian fare. Inventive dishes such as peppered halibut with sweet potato hash are artistically presented. Excellent wine list. Weekend jazz brunch. $$$

The Red Lion

38470 Boulder Canyon, Highway 119
Tel: 303/442-9368

Well known for its wonderful wild game selections, such as marinated boar tenderloin to venison satay, the Red Lion also serves excellent steaks, seafood, and imaginative specials, including pecan-crusted lamb and coconut crusted red snapper. Extensive wine list, with many wines available by the glass – and good service. The hexagonal dining room is surrounded by windows with lovely views out to the mountains. $$$

Right: Rock Bottom Brewery, 16th St Mall, Downtown Denver

Walnut Street Brewery
1123 Walnut Street
Tel: 303/447-1345
Set in a century-old brick building, this spacious brewpub serves great food in a fun environment. Pub favorites include smoked fish and chips, buffalo *fajitas*, and excellent vegetarian enchiladas. Also sandwich platters, pasta, salads, and dinner entrees from steaks to chicken. $–$$

Dushanbe Teahouse
1770 13th Street
Tel: 303/442-4993
Delicious 'world cuisine' from Persian tamarind shrimp to Tibetan Kongpo beef are served in this enchanting, ornate teahouse from Tajikistan *(see p51)*. $–$$

Golden
The Golden Ram
822 13th Street
Tel: 303/279-6011
Nostalgic café, filled with memorabilia from Golden's past. Good breakfasts and lunches. Closed for dinner. $

Old Capitol Grill
1122 Washington Street
Tel: 303/279-6390
Lively spot for salads, ribs, and chicken. Outdoor deck along Golden's main street. $–$$

Table Mountain Inn
1310 Washington Avenue
Tel: 303/271-0110
Casual restaurant with adobe-style decor and excellent Southwestern cuisine. Wild game and fish specials in season. Patio dining available. Bar. $$

Winter Park
The Shed
78672 US 40 (town center)
Tel: 970/726-9912
This is a bright, fun place to enjoy giant Margaritas and good Mexican food, as well as house specials like wild boar, steak, and salmon. $$

Fontenot's Cajun Cafe
Park Plaza, US 40 (town center)
Tel: 970/726-4021
Excellent Louisiana-style fare, from bayou shrimp to Creole jambalaya to fried catfish. Meat and pasta dishes, too. $$

Carver's Bakery Cafe
Downtown, off Vasquez Road behind Cooper Creek Square
Tel: 970/726-8202
Favorite local hang-out known for fabulous breakfasts and bakery goods, and healthy lunch fare. $

Rudi's Deli
Park Plaza, US 40 (town center)
Tel: 970/726-8955
Great deli sandwiches to eat on the deck or take-out. $

Beaver Creek
Vista Brasserie
48 East Beaver Creek Boulevard, Avon
Tel: 303/949-3366
Vista Brasserie is a lively spot for good food, from pasta, pizza, and salads to delicious meat and fish entrees. $$

Nederland
Tungsten Grill
Downtown Nederland
Tel: 303/258-9231
Live music, microbrews, and an outdoor sundeck make this a lively place for lunch or dinner. Daily specials are good value. $–$$

Above: Dushanbe Teahouse, Boulder
Right: blowin' free – brass band at the AT&T LoDo music festival

NIGHTLIFE

Long before it had a school or a hospital, Denver in the 1870s had several theaters, one of which boasted sell-out performances of *Macbeth*. Today, more people buy tickets for performing arts than for professional sports events in the city. In addition to the Denver Performing Arts Complex, there are some 30 theaters and over 100 movie theaters in the metro area.

Tickets can usually be purchased at the venues, or by phone through **Ticketmaster** (tel: 303/830-TIXS or 719/520-9090), **TicketMan** (tel: 303/430-1111 or 800/200-TIXS) or **TicketWeb** (tel: 303/830-4TIX or 800/965-4827). Ticketmaster outlets include Foley's and Blockbuster Music. Tickets for most concerts can be purchased through **Rocky Mountain Teleseat** at King Soopers supermarkets (tel: 800/444-SEAT).

Denver has an exuberant nightlife. The hottest late-night spot is Lower Downtown, or LoDo, where more than 90 bars, clubs, and restaurants are located almost door-to-door. The lines are blurred between bars, clubs, and even restaurants. Some bars have live music some or all nights of the week, others have dance floors, and some of the trendiest bars can be found in restaurants, which may also offer live music.

The legal drinking age is 21. Bars and nightclubs are generally open until 2am.

The free weekly tabloid *Westword* is the most comprehensive source of entertainment listings. The *Denver Post* and *Rocky Mountain News* have entertainment pages in their Friday editions, as does the *Boulder Daily Camera*. *Where Denver* is a listings magazine distributed at hotels. *Boulder Weekly* has entertainment listings for Boulder.

Denver Performing Arts Complex
14th Street and Curtis (Center box office)
Tel: 303/93-4100
The Plex covers four city blocks and comprises eight theaters, seating over 10,000 people. It is the second-largest such center in the country, after NYC's Lincoln Center. Its venues include:

Auditorium Theater
This historic 1908 proscenium house became the country's first municipal auditorium. Home to the Colorado Ballet and Broadway touring shows.

Boettcher Concert Hall
Unique 2,634-seat concert hall in-the-round, home to the CSO.

Garner Galleria Theater
Intimate cabaret-style entertainment and long-running musical shows.

Temple Hoyne Buell Theater
State-of-the-art 2,830-seat house, home to the Colorado Ballet, Cleo Parker Robinson Dance, Opera Colorado, Broadway touring shows, and other musical/theatrical productions.

Helen Bonfils Theater Complex
Four small theaters for intimate and experimental productions: The Stage, The Space, The Ricketson, and The Source. Home to the Denver Center Theater Company, Denver Center Theater Academy, National Theater Conservatory, and Denver Center Attractions.

Theater
The Avenue Theater
2119 E 17th Avenue
Tel: 303/321-5925
Top-rated theater; often produces comedies.

The Changing Scene
1527 1/2 Champa Street
Tel: 303/893-5775
Denver's oldest independent theater, producing world premieres, original dramas, dance, and other events.

Arts Theater of the West
721 Santa Fe Drive
Tel: 303/595-3800
Comprises ttwo theaters and stages well-known plays, musicals, and original works.

Germinal Stage Denver
2450 W 44th Avenue
Tel: 303/455-7108
Highly regarded small theater producing traditional and experimental plays.

Opera
Opera Colorado
Tel: 303/778-1500
www.operacolorado.org
Denver's premier grand opera company stages three operas a year, attracting stars such as Placido Domingo. Its major season in Boettcher Concert Hall is in April and May, with other presentations in The Buell.

Central City Opera House
Eureka Street
Tel: 303/292-6700 or 800/851-8175
www.www-central-cityopera.com
Three operas are presented during the summer at this historic Victorian opera house.

Classical Music
Colorado Symphony Orchestra
Tel: 303/292-5566
www.coloradosymphony.com
Performs classical, pops, and family concerts at Boettcher Concert Hall (Sept–June), as well as summer concerts in City, Washington, and Sloan Lake parks.

Dance
Colorado Ballet
Tel: 303/837-8888
www.coloradoballet.org
Classical ballet company with fall, winter, and spring seasons at the Buell Theater.

Cleo Parker Robinson Dance
Tel: 303/295-1759
A multi-cultural dance organization that performs at the Buell Theater.

Film
Mayan Theater
110 Broadway
Tel: 303/744-6796
Landmark theater showing intelligent films.

The Bluebird Theater
3317 East Colfax
Tel: 303/322-2308
Shows movie classics and musicals on Sunday nights. Live music Wed–Sat.

Concert Venues
Pepsi Center
Off Speer Boulevard and Auraria Parkway
Tel: 303/405-8555 (information)
or 303/ 405-1111 (box office)
State-of-the-art venue for large concerts.

Red Rocks Amphitheater
I-70 West to Morrison Exit
Tel: 303/458 4850
or 303/640-7334 (recorded info)
Spectacular venue. Summer concerts range from symphonies to rock, jazz, and pop.

Above: the Colorado Ballet performing *Carmina Burama* at the Denver Performing Arts Complex

Paramount Theater
1631 Glenarm Place
Tel: 303/534-8336
Fabulous Art-Deco theater presents pop concerts, top-name acts, and other events.

The Ogden Theater
935 East Colfax Street
Tel: 303/830-2525
Local and national bands.

Festivals
Colorado Shakespeare Festival
Boulder
Tel: 303/492-0554
Held outdoors at the Mary Rippon Theater on the University campus; June–Aug.

Colorado Music Festival
Boulder
Tel: 303/449-1397
www.coloradomusicfest.com
Classical concerts four nights a week for seven weeks, beginning in June, at the open-air Chautauqua Auditorium.

Colorado Dance Festival
Boulder
Tel: 303/442-7666
Dance companies and artists from several continents. Program starts in July.

Colorado Performing Arts Festival
Denver Performing Arts Complex
Tel: 303/640-2678
Dance, theater, music, opera and more at this two-day event in late Sept/early Oct.

Denver International Film Festival
Tel: 303/595-FILM
Various venues (Oct).

Comedy Clubs
Comedy Works
1226 15th Street
Tel: 303/595-3637
Famous/up-and-coming comedy acts, Wed–Sun, Tues amateur night. Minimum age 21.

Chicken Lips Comedy Theater
1624 Market Street, Suite 301
Tel: 303/534-4440
Improvisational satire and political parody.

Brewpubs and Pool Halls
Wynkoop Brewing Company
18th and Wynkoop Street
Tel: 303/297-2700
Characterful brewpub, with 25 pool tables upstairs. Great beer, good food. The Impulse Theater downstairs features music, comedy, and cabaret.

Red Rock Brewing Company
1001 16th Street (16th St Mall)
Tel: 303/534-7616
Huge brewpub and pool hall with great outdoor dining and people-watching.

Breckenridge Brewery
2220 Blake Street
Tel: 303/297-3644
Brews, billiards, and pub fare; blues jam on Tues and live music on patio at weekends.

Walnut Brewery
1123 Walnut Street, Boulder
Tel: 303/447-1345
Friendly brew-pub with great food.

Shakespeare's
2375 15th Street
Tel: 303/433-6000
Serious pool hall with many tables, including billiards. Live jazz on Sunday afternoons.

Live Music
Boulder Theater
2034 14th Street, Boulder
Tel: 303/786-7030
Headliner gigs with top jazz entertainers.

El Chapultepec
1962 Market Street
Tel: 303/295-9126
Old-fashioned, tiny, authentic jazz club.

Trios Enoteca
1730 Wynkoop Street
Tel: 303/293-2887
Elegant nightspot. Live jazz five nights a week.

Herman's Hideaway
1578 South Broadway
Tel: 303/777-5840
National acts range from rock to reggae. Booking advised

CALENDAR OF EVENTS

Denver is the cultural capital of Rocky Mountain West, and major events here draw visitors from hundreds of miles. In summer, there are music festivals and special events every weekend, either in the city or the surrounding region. Many festivals celebrate Denver's rich ethnic background. Specific dates for many of the following events vary from year to year. The Denver Metro Convention & Visitors Bureau *(see page 88)* can provide exact dates. Also see 'Nightlife' *(page 75)* for long-running cultural events.

January
National Western Stock Show and Rodeo, Denver Coliseum: the world's premier livestock show where more than 10,000 animals are shown and sold, and one of the biggest rodeos in the country.

The Annual Colorado Cowboy Poetry Gathering, Arvada Center for the Arts and Humanities: tall tales and Western humor as regional poets give three evening performances in mid-Jan.

February
Buffalo Bill's Birthday, the Buckhorn Exchange Restaurants: held in one of Bill's favorite watering holes and the Buffalo Bill Museum on Lookout Mountain, with lookalike contests, entertainment, and other festivities around Feb 26.

March
St Patrick's Day Parade: this Rocky Mountain version of St Paddy's Day, with stagecoaches, horses, and marching bands in downtown Denver, is the second largest in the country after New York City's.

Denver March Pow Wow, Denver Coliseum: dancing, drumming, costumes, and food at one of the largest Native American gatherings, with tribes from across North America.

April
Easter Sunrise Service, Red Rocks Park: inspirational service in this natural outdoor arena carved out of red sandstone rocks; nondenominational.

May
Cinco de Mayo, Civic Center Park: Colorado's largest Hispanic celebration, with *mariachi* bands, dancers, entertainment, crafts, and fantastic food, held May 5.

Kinetic Conveyance Challenge, Boulder Reservoir: people-powered crafts race over land and water in this wacky event, judged on creativity, costumes, spirit, and speed.

Bolder Boulder: a Memorial Day tradition, this race through the streets of Boulder attracts runners from around the world, with music and a great party atmosphere on the sidelines.

June
CHUN Capitol Hill People's Fair: Denver celebrates the start of summer in Civic Center Park with six outdoor stages of continuous entertainment, art and crafts, and food.

Renaissance Festival, Larkspur: costumed characters re-create the Renaissance in a 16th-century village with jousting contests, music, and crafts; held in a forest south of Denver, every weekend from mid-June until end-July.

Juneteenth, Five Points neighborhood: parade, Gospel extravaganza, entertainment, and exotic food, to commemorate the end of slavery in Texas.

Above: Native American Pow Wow

Platte River Rendezvous, Confluence Park: week-long Mountain Man festival with costumed actors to celebrate founding of Denver.

US West International BuskerFest: downtown Denver becomes street performer capital of the world during three-day gathering of jugglers, mimes, musicians, and magicians.

July
Cherry Creek Arts Festival: Great fine-arts and crafts exhibition, with every type of craft from watercolor and photography to jewelry-making. Entertainment. Top restaurants present signature dishes on Culinary Row.

Independence Day: excellent July 4 spectacle in Avon, near Vail, with fireworks synchronized to music and free outdoor concert.

Confluence Concerts: free summer concert series on the riverfront at Confluence Park, featuring jazz, blues, and classical.

LoDo Music Festival: Lower Downtown has people dancing in the streets. Top musicians on four outdoor stages.

Buffalo Bill Days, Golden: parade, burro race, Wild West show, and other activities to honor the region's favorite frontiersman.

Winter Park Jazz Festival: national names perform at this two-day outdoor event.

KBCO World Class Rockfest, Winter Park: national acts and up-and-coming regional bands perform at two-day outdoor concert.

August
Riverfest, Confluence and Commons parks: the Denver Duck Derby and the Great Platt River Relay Race are among the events.

Rocky Mountain Wine and Food Festival, Winter Park: wine and beer tasting, with food prepared by Colorado's finest chefs.

September
Festival of Mountain & Plain: A Taste of Colorado: free entertainment, rides, and great food from 75 of state's best restaurants; held Labor Day weekend in Civic Center Park.

Right: Ostriches Neighborhood Watch Stilts at Cherry Creek Arts Festival

Longs Peak Scottish-Irish Highland Festival, Estes Park: one of the largest Celtic festivals in the US, with bagpipe bands, Irish dancing, folk music and Highland games.

Oktoberfest, Larimer Square: beer, bratwurst, dancing and German oompah bands, held on Denver's oldest street.

October
Colorado Performing Arts Festival *(see page 75)*.

Great American Beer Festival, Currigan Exhibition Hall: the nation's largest beer festival, with samples of over 1,700 lagers, stouts, ales, chili beers, and designer brews.

Denver International Film Festival *(see page 75)*.

November
Rocky Mountain Book Festival, Denver Merchandise Mart: author signings, storytellers, celebrity book auctions, and displays.

Winterfest, Larimer Square: Santa's workshops, live reindeer, carolers, tuba concerts; every weekend through Dec.

December
Parade of Lights: themed floats, marching bands, and giant balloons in downtown parade.

Wild Lights, Denver Zoo: lighting displays include huge animals created by light.

Blossoms of Light, Denver Botanic Gardens: thousands of twinkling lights decorate the gardens, many forming gigantic flowers.

Practical
Information

GETTING THERE

By Air

The distinctive white peaks of the **Denver International Airport** (DIA) terminal billow up from the surrounding flat plain. It lies 24 miles (38km) northeast of Downtown on Peña Boulevard and can be reached via the marked exit off I-70. It has one huge terminal with three concourses, and is served by 20 airlines with daily non-stop flights from many cities, including London and Frankfurt. Facilities include a bureau de change (24 hours), ATMs, tourist information, restaurants, and retail outlets. For general information tel: 303/342-2000 or www.flydenver.com

From the Airport

The cheapest way into the city is on RTD's SkyRide buses (tel: 303/299-6000, www.RTD-Denver.com). They run hourly between 4am and midnight, with fares between $4 and $8, 29 metro-area stops. Several shuttle companies provide transportation in 10-passenger vans. These include SuperShuttle (tel: 303/370-1300), which offers residential service, Airporter (tel: 303/227-0000), and Wolf Express (tel: 303/333-4000). The trip to Downtown takes about 40 minutes and costs around $20. There are taxi ranks outside the baggage claim area. The average fare to Downtown at the time of writing is around $40. The Denver Visitors Guide lists several limousine companies, which must be booked in advance.

All the major car rental firms have desks in the arrivals hall, including Avis (tel: 800/331-1212), Budget (tel: 303/342-7212), Dollar (tel: 800/800-4000), and Thrifty (tel: 800/367-2277). Allow extra time for picking up and dropping off your rental car, as the actual parking lot is some distance away from the main terminal, reached by frequent shuttle buses.

By Rail

Denver's **Union Station** at 1701 Wynkoop Street is on Amtrak's main east–west routes from Chicago to Seattle, San Francisco, and Los Angeles, and there are three arrivals per day. The Denver Amtrak ticket office has recorded information about arrivals and departures (tel: 303/534-2812). For information on Amtrak routes and fares, tel: 800/USA RAIL (www.amtrak.com).

By Road

Denver lies at the intersection of two major interstate highways: I-70, which runs east–west from Pittsburgh through St Louis and on into Utah, and I-25 which runs south from Wyoming through New Mexico to El Paso, Texas. It also connects with the coast-to-coast I-80 route via I-76.

TRAVEL ESSENTIALS

Visas and Passports

You will need a full, valid passport for entry into the United States, and some visitors also need a visa. British and Canadian citizens, plus travelers from some European countries, do not need visas if they are staying for less than 90 days and have a return ticket.

Customs

Everyone entering the country must go through customs, whether or not they have anything to declare. You can freely import

Left: Light Rail Train and mural
Right: Platte Valley trolley

Read ↓

up to $10,000; amounts greater than this must be declared. Adults may bring in 1 liter (or quart) of alcohol; 200 cigarettes or 50 cigars (Cuban prohibited) or 4.4 pounds (2kg) of tobacco; and gifts valued at under $4,100 (gifts of higher value are subject to duty and taxes).

Weather

Denver has around 300 days of sunshine a year. While the city does get snow in the winter, temperatures are much milder than in the mountains. Summer is hot but with low humidity, and there can be sudden afternoon thundershowers.

The sun is much stronger at Denver's high altitude, so protect yourself with sunscreen, sunglasses, and a hat. Spring and fall weather is unpredictable, with unexpected snowstorms or heat waves. At any season, Colorado weather can change quickly, so be prepared.

January is the coldest month, with average highs and lows of 44°F (6.6°C) and 16°F (-9°C) respectively. July is the hottest month, with average highs of 87°F (30.5°C) and average lows of 59°F (15°C). May is generally the rainiest month.

Clothing

In Denver dress casually in all but the most upscale restaurants. Because of the sudden weather changes, layering is best in Colorado.

Bring garments that you can layer on top of each other, and add or shed as necessary. If you're heading for the mountains, bear in mind that temperatures drop sharply at higher altitudes. Bring a waterproof jacket, windbreaker, and/or warm sweater. Comfortable walking shoes are a must, and hiking boots or sneakers are the best footwear in the mountains. In winter you will need a warm jacket and gloves.

Electricity

The US standard is 110 volts, 60 cycle AC. Plugs have two flat prongs.

Time Differences

Denver is on Mountain Standard Time, which is GMT -7 hours. It is 2 hours behind New York City and 1 hour ahead of Los Angeles. Daylight Savings Time (summer time) is observed.

GETTING ACQUAINTED

Geography

Denver, the mile-high city, sits tall in the saddle at 5,280ft (1,609 meters). It rests on the high plains of what is called the Front Range, at the base of the eastern foothills of the Rocky Mountains. It is the biggest city in a 600-mile (965-km) radius.

While this position makes for great beauty and pleasant climate, it also causes a temperature inversion as cold air sweeping in from the high mountains acts as a lid, holding down the hotter fumes from car exhaust and industry, creating Denver's bane, the 'brown cloud.' The mountains also shield precipitation, creating dry conditions on the Front Range.

Population

The Denver metro area has a multicultural population of 2.1 million – and it's still growing. About 20 percent of the people have Hispanic ancestry, 13 percent African-American, 2 percent Asian and 1 percent Native American. Many new Denver residents are relocating from California due to tax laws, overcrowding, and other social problems on the affluent West Coast.

MONEY MATTERS

Currency

American currency uses the decimal system of dollars and cents (100 cents to the dollar). There are $100, $50, $20, $10, $5, and $1 bills (notes), and $1, 25¢ (quarter), 10¢ (dime), 5¢ (nickle) and 1¢ (penny) coins. The $1 and 25¢ coins are similar in size, so count your change.

Above: Cinco de Mayo Parade, Downtown Denver

Changing Money

Denver International Airport has a 24-hour currency exchange booth at the main terminal. You can change cash and traveler's checks at the American Express Travel Service, Qwest Tower, 555 17th Street (tel: 303/383-5050) and Thomas Cook Currency Services, 299 Detroit Street (tel: 303/333-5714), open Mon–Fri 9am–6pm, Sat 10am–5pm. Downtown banks that handle foreign exchange include Bank One, Colorado, and US Bank, both on 17th Street; KeyBank and Norwest Bank Colorado, both with several metro locations. Be sure to bring photo identification. You may have difficulty converting foreign currency and traveler's checks outside the city.

Traveler's Checks

It is a good idea to carry American dollar traveler's checks, as they can be exchanged without converting and incurring commission fees. Well-known brands of traveler's checks such as American Express can be used like cash in hotels, restaurants, and larger chain stores, as long as you have photo identification such as a passport or driver's license.

ATMS

ATMs (cash machines) are abundant Downtown, often located outside major bank buildings. In the suburbs you will find them in shopping malls and supermarkets. Most machines now add on a charge of $2–$4 per transaction, although this may not apply to non-US bank cards. The charges are stated on the outside of the machine.

Credit Cards

Well-known credit cards, such as Visa, MasterCard, Discover Card, and American Express are accepted in all but the smallest shops. Most cards can be used to withdraw cash from an ATM (although there will be a fee), or to obtain cash advances over the counter at a bank.

Tipping

Tipping in the US is customary and expected. Tip porters at airports and hotel bellhops about $1 per bag. A doorman should be tipped if he unloads or parks your car, usually $1 or so. Tip chambermaids if you stay several days in a small hotel.

A tip of 15–20 percent of the bill before tax is the going rate for waiters, waitresses, bar staff, taxi drivers, and hair dressers. In some restaurants the tip or a service charge is included in the bill if it is for a large group.

Taxes

Denver has a 7½ percent sales tax, which is added to the stated price of goods at the check-out counter. There are higher taxes for lodging and car rental.

GETTING AROUND

Light Rail

Denver's light rail service, operated by the Regional Transportation District (RTD), runs along a central line through Downtown, from 30th Avenue and Downing Street in the north, through Downtown, to the Auraria Campus and on to Santa Fe Drive and Mineral Avenue in Littleton. The Downtown stops are at the 16th Street Mall and California going south, and 16th and Stout going north. Rail cars are comfortable and air-conditioned.

Buses

Shuttle buses running up and down the 16th Street Mall are free and run daily at frequent intervals until 1am. RTD operates local and express buses throughout the metro area; exact change is required. There are also regional buses that run to Boulder and other locations; the fare is very reasonable. For information on bus routes to and from your destination, call RTD on 303/299 6000.

You can buy tokens, ticket books, and monthly passes at supermarkets and other locations. A day pass, good for all local bus routes as well as the light rail, is good value. For passes, schedules, and route information, stop by the Civic Center Bus Terminal at 16th and Broadway, or the Market Street Station at 16th and Market.

Cultural Connection Trolley

From mid-May through Labor Day weekend (early Sept), RTD runs a special trolley that stops near most of the city's popular attractions at roughly half-hour intervals. Tickets are good value and valid all day from 9.30am to 6.30pm. The pass is also valid on local buses and the light rail. You can buy tickets on the bus or at the terminals listed above.

Taxis

You can occasionally flag down a cab in downtown Denver, but generally you need to call ahead. There are taxi ranks outside major hotels and at the bus and train stations. Try any of the following:
Zone Cab: 303/444-8888
Yellow Cab: 303/777-7777
Metro Taxi: 303/333-3333

Cars

Outside the downtown area, it is easiest to get around with a car. Driving is on the right, and seat belts are required. You can make a right turn on a red light, provided there is nothing coming, there are no pedestrians in the crosswalk, or no sign prohibiting it. Speed limits are generally 25mph (40 kph) in business districts, 30mph (48kph) in residential areas and 55 or 65mph (88 or 140kph) on highways, as posted.

The peak rush hours are 7–9am and 4–6pm, when traffic is usually bumper-to-

bumper. Beware of carpool lanes on I-25, US 36, and Santa Fe Drive – there must be at least two passengers to use these lanes. If you're returning from the mountains on I-70 and Highway 285, avoid late afternoon and evening on Sundays or holiday Mondays, when traffic is horrific.

Parking

Parking in Downtown Denver is expensive. Prices are higher the closer you are to the center, so look for parking lots on the outskirts of Downtown. Parking lots in LoDo, particularly those near Coors Field, double their rates when there's a baseball game. Parking meters have a limit of two hours.

HOURS AND HOLIDAYS

Business Hours

Most banks open Mon-Fri 9am–5pm, and some are also open on Saturday mornings. Business hours are generally 8 or 9am–5 or 6pm.

Shopping Hours

Most stores are open from 9 or 9.30am–6 or 7pm in downtown locations, and until 9 or 10pm in shopping malls; malls may close earlier on weekends.

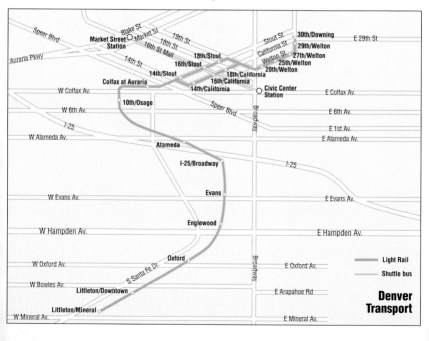

Public Holidays

Most federal, state, and municipal offices, schools, and banks are closed on public holidays *(see below)*. Some holidays are celebrated on the closest Monday, in order to give people a long weekend. Some banks and businesses also close on Lincoln's Birthday (Feb 12) and Good Friday (before Easter Sunday). Except for Christmas and New Year, many attractions are open on holidays.

New Year's Day – Jan 1
Martin Luther King Day – mid Jan
President's Day – late Feb
Easter Sunday – Mar or Apr
Memorial Day – late May
Independence Day – July 4
Labor Day – early Sept
Columbus Day – mid Oct
Veterans Day – mid Nov
Thanksgiving Day – fourth Thur in Nov
Christmas Day – Dec 25

ACCOMMODATIONS

Accommodations in Denver and the surrounding area generally represent good value, whether you want a luxury hotel or budget accommodations. Downtown and central Denver feature grand historic hotels and chic new boutique hotels, in addition to motel chains. Boulder and other towns have properties of great character, including bed-and-breakfast accommodations, while Winter Park, Vail and other mountain areas have condos and efficiency apartments with kitchen facilities. For complete accommodations listings, contact tourist information *(see page 88)*.

Price categories are for a standard double room, and some hotels have executive suites which will be higher. Tax, including a 13.5 percent state occupancy tax, is added to the bill. Breakfast is not usually included except in B&Bs, although many motels now offer a complimentary continental breakfast. Be sure and ask about special offers, as leading hotels often have special weekend rates.

$$$$ – over $200
$$$ – $150–200
$$ – $100–150
$ – under $100

Right: the Brown Palace Hotel is a Denver landmark

Denver

Warwick Hotel
1776 Grant Street, 80203
Tel: 303/861-2000 or 800/525-2888
Fax: 303/839-8504
Website: www.warwickhotels.com
Email: warwickres@aol.com
Deluxe, European-style hotel with 206 large rooms with balconies, some with mountain views. Heated rooftop pool and sundeck, French/American restaurant. $$$$

Brown Palace Hotel
321 17th Street, 80202
Tel: 303/297-3111 or 800/321-2599
Fax: 303/312-5900
Website: www.brownpalace.com
Brown Palace Hotel, the grand dame of Denver hotels is a landmark in its own right with its gorgeous atrium lobby *(see page 29)*, Victorian charm and excellent service. The 230 rooms are elegantly appointed, with soothing colors, plush furnishings, and amenities, and there are also beautiful suites. Historical tours highlight the hotel's history. Afternoon tea is served in the lobby, and there are three good restaurants including the casual Ship's Tavern and the distinguished Palace Arms *(see page 69)*, plus a cigar bar. $$$–$$$$

Hotel Monaco
1717 Champa Street, 80202
Tel: 303/296-1717
or 800/397-5380 (reservations)
Fax: 303/ 296-1818
Website: www.monaco-denver.com
Email: reservations@monaco-denver.com
This hip, high-style boutique hotel in downtown Denver is a luxurious urban retreat. The 189 rooms and 32 suites are designer-

decorated with bright printed and striped furnishings, and each room even has a pet goldfish. Many thoughtful touches, as well as excellent amenities, such as a fitness center, valet parking, complimentary 'altitude adjustment' wine hour in the lobby lounge. The Renaissance Aveda Spa offers fabulous facials, massages, and spa treatments. Panzano's restaurant *(see page 70)* serves outstanding Italian cuisine. $$$–$$$$

Adam's Mark
1550 Court Place, 80202
Tel: 303/893-3333 or 800/444-2326
Fax: 303/626-2542
Website: www.adamsmark.com
Huge, stylish hotel at the top of the 16th Street Mall. 1,225 well-appointed guest rooms and suites, with complimentary health club, heated pool, coin laundry, parking, and other services. $$$

Oxford Hotel
1600 17th Street, 80202
Tel: 303/628-5400
Fax: 303/628-5413
Website: www.theoxfordhotel.com
Historic 80-room hotel in LoDo, built in 1891 by the same architect who designed the wonderful Brown Palace *(see page 83)*. Luxuriously furnished with European antiques, all rooms have great natural light. The piano from the old Tabor Grand Opera House resides in the lobby amid beautiful Victorian decor. The Art-Deco Cruise Room bar adjoins the lobby. $$$

Teatro Hotel
1100 14th Street, 80202
Tel: 303/228-1100
Fax: 303/228-1101
Website: www.wyndham.com
In the historic Tramway Tower building of 1911, opposite the Denver Performing Arts Complex. Theatrical costumes, photographs, and artworks decorate the public areas. 116 rooms with contemporary decor and amenities such as fax, printer, internet access, CD player. Plus fitness center, restaurants. $$$

Courtyard by Marriott
934 16th Street, 80202
Tel: 303/571-1114 or 888/249-1810
Fax: 303/ 571-1141
Handsomely restored Victorian building in Downtown, with atrium lobby and fireplaces. 181 rooms of varying size, with amenities for business travelers. $$–$$$

Embassy Suites
1881 Curtis Street, 80202
Tel: 303/297-8888 or (800) 733-3366
Fax: 303/298-1103
Website: www.ESDENT.com
337 rooms in spacious one- and two-bedroom suites. Nicely decorated with refrigerator, microwave, wet bar, and other amenities. Complementary breakfast. Convenient for LoDo. $$

LoDo Inn
1612 Wazee, 80202
Tel: 303/572-3300 or 877/LODO INN
Fax: 303/623-0773
Home comforts in an elegant B&B. Amenities for business travelers, complementary beverages, snacks, wine, and cheese. 14 rooms. $$–$$$

Loews Giorgio Hotel
4150 East Mississippi Avenue, 80246
Tel: 303/782-9300
or 800/345-9172 (reservations)
Fax: 303/758-0283
Website: www.loewshotels.com
Richly appointed hotel near Cherry Creek Shopping Center, with classic Italian decor and Renaissance-style murals. 187 rooms and 19 suites with amenities, fitness center, library, and Tuscany Restaurant. $$–$$$

Above: the Oxford Hotel in LoDo

Lumber Baron Inn
2555 West 37th Avenue, 80211
Tel: 303/477-8205 or 800/697-6552
Fax: 303/477-0269
Website: www.lumberbaron.com
Email: stay@lumberbaron.com
Built by a Scottish lumber baron in 1890, this grand home was near demolition before being renovated as a luxury bed & breakfast. Beautiful carved wood staircase and five romantic rooms decorated with Victorian antiques. In the historic Highlands district just west of Downtown. $$-$$$$

La Quinta Inn – Cherry Creek
1975 South Colorado Boulevard, 80222
Tel: 303/758-8886 or 800/531-5900
Fax: 303/756-2711
129 stylish rooms, some suites and family units. Heated pool, free continental breakfast. $-$$

Queen Anne Bed & Breakfast Inn
2147 Tremont Place
Tel: 303/296-6666 or 800/432-INNS
Fax: 303/296-2151
14 rooms and four suites in two romantic, downtown Victorian houses, opposite a quiet park. Themed rooms with elegant period furnishings, one with a fireplace. $-$$$

Red Lion Hotel Denver Central
4040 Quebec Street, 80216
Tel: 303/321-6666
 or 800/RED-LION (reservations)
Fax: 303/355-7412
Website: www.redlion.com
This beautifully renovated hotel near the airport has a comfortable lobby with hardwood floors, double-sided fireplace, and leather sofas. 303 spacious rooms with iron, coffee maker, and other amenities. Health club, pool, hot tub, coin laundry, business center. $-$$

Westin Tabor Center
1672 Lawrence, 80202
Tel: 303/572-9100 or 800/WESTIN1
Fax: 303/572-7288
Website: www.westin.com
420 well-appointed rooms, adjoining the shops and restaurants of the Tabor Center on the 16th Street Mall. Heated pool, sauna, whirlpool, and racquetball court. $-$$

Out of Town
Boulder
Hotel Boulderado
2115 13th Street, 80302
Tel: 303/442-4344 or 800/433-4344
Fax: 303/443-7035
Website: www.boulderado.com
Email: info@boulderado.com
Named for the words 'Boulder' and 'Colorado' so that no guest would forget where he'd stayed, this wonderful hotel is a city landmark, opened in 1909. A stained-glass atrium ceiling and cantilevered cherry staircase are highlights of the stunning Victorian lobby. 160 rooms and suites, those in the original building have the most character, with antiques and period reproductions; plush modern annex. Business center, health club passes, Q's restaurant *(see page 71),* and Catacombs Blues Bar, the oldest in town. A gem. $$$

Alps Boulder Canyon Inn
38619 Boulder Canyon Drive, 80302
Tel: 303/444-5445 or 800/414-2577
Fax: 303/444-5522
Email: alpsinn@aol.com
This idyllic hideaway in Boulder Canyon features large, luxury rooms in a beautifully restored 1870s log inn, a former stagecoach stop, and massive fireplaces in the lounge and dining area. Each of the 12 rooms is unique, with ceiling fan and fireplace; many have patios or porches with mountain views, and special features such as antique bathtubs, Jacuzzi baths, antiques, and carved wood mantelpieces. Delicious gourmet breakfast and evening dessert included. Fishing, bicycles, hiking trails. $$-$$$$

Best Western Boulder Inn
770 28th Street, 80303
Tel: 303/449-3800
 or 800/233-8469 (reservations)
Fax: 303/402-9118
Website: www.boulderinn.com
Email: boulderinn@aol.com
Comfortable, quiet, rooms with all amenities, adjacent to the University of Colorado. Outdoor pool, indoor hot tub and sauna, complementary continental breakfast and health club passes. Facilities for business travelers. Restaurant and sports bar. $-$$

practical information

Golden
The Golden Hotel
800 11th Street, 80401
Tel: 303/279-0100 or 800/233-7214
Fax: 303/279-9353
Website: www.golden-hotel.com
Email: star@golden-hotel.com
Western ambience and decor in this well-furnished, town-center hotel, built in 1999 on the banks of Clear Creek. Has 62 comfortable rooms and suites, with many amenities. $

Table Mountain Inn
1310 Washington Avenue, 80401
Tel: 303/277-9898 or 800/762-9898
Fax: 303/27100298
Adobe-style hotel in the town center. Rooms and public areas are decorated with Southwestern flair. 74 rooms range from cozy with private patios to luxurious suites with fireplace, jetted tubs, and balconies. Business amenities, good restaurant serving the local cuisine. $–$$

Nederland
Sundance Cafe & Lodge
Highway 119, 80466
(1 mile south of Nederland)
Tel: 303/258-3797
This is a great little mountain get-away, west of Boulder on the way to Rocky Mountain National Park. Offers 12 cozy rooms, simply but sweetly decorated. Good café. Recreation activities available. $

Vail and Beaver Creek
Hyatt Regency Beaver Creek Resort & Spa
PO Box 1595, Avon, 81620
Tel: 970/ 949-1234 or 800/55-HYATT
Fax: 970/949-4164
Website: www.beavercreek.hyatt.com
Rocky Mountain chic abounds at this elegant but relaxed hotel at the base of the ski lifts, adjoining the pedestrian village. The 276 rooms are beautifully decorated with lodge-style knotty pine furnishings, fluffy comforters, oversize pillows and large marble baths. All have mountain or valley views. Public areas include wall-sized fireplaces and cozy alcoves. The spa features outdoor and indoor swimming pools and five whirlpools, and a range of spa treatments. Low-season specials make this luxury hotel surprisingly affordable even for those on a budget. $–$$$$

Black Bear Inn of Vail
2405 Elliott Road, Vail, 81657
Tel: 970/476-1304
Fax: 970/ 476-0433
Website: www.vail.net/blackbear
Bed & breakfast in a handcrafted log cabin, set along Gore Creek. 12 rooms with private baths, down comforters. Hearty mountain breakfasts, afternoon snacks, hot tub. $$–$$$$

Winter Park
The Vintage Hotel
100 Winter Park Drive, PO Box 1369, 80482
Tel: 970/726-8801
or 800/472-7017 (reservations)
Fax: 970/726-9230
With a beautiful mountain setting halfway between the town and the ski resort, this handsome hotel is excellent value, especially off season. The 118 rooms are all comfortably appointed, and range from traditional hotel rooms to suites to studios with kitchenettes and fireplaces and fold-down hideaway beds. Library, restaurant, and bar, deli, sauna, outdoor heated pool and hot tub, laundry facilities. $–$$$

Motels
Most of the major national hotel and motel chains have accommodations in Denver and out of town, priced in the budget-to-mod-

Left: Vail village

erate price categories. Contact the following central reservations numbers for information and bookings.

Best Western, tel: 1-800-528-1234
Comfort Inn, tel: 1-800-221-2222
Days Inn, tel: 1-800-325-2525
Holiday Inn, tel: 1-800-HOLIDAY; website: www.holiday-inn.com
Howard Johnson, tel: 1-800-654-4656
La Quinta Motor Inn, tel: 1-800-531-5900
Quality Inn, tel: 1-800-228-5151
Sleep Inn, tel: 1-800-221-2222; website: www.sunbursthospitality.com
Super 8 Motels, tel: 1-800-800-8000
Travelodge, tel: 1-800-578-7878

Camping

There are campgrounds at 40 Colorado State Parks. For campground reservations tel: 800/678-2267. Or contact the tourist information center for campground listings.

Hostels

Denver International Youth Hostel
630 East 16th Avenue, 80203
Tel: 303/832-9996
Fax: 303/861-1376
Website: www.youthhostels.com/denver

Hostel of the Rocky Mountains
1530 Downing Street, 80218
Tel: 303/861-7777

HEALTH AND EMERGENCIES

It is essential to have health insurance when traveling in the US, as all medical and dental services are extremely expensive.

High altitude living takes a little getting used to. A few people experience shortness of breath in Denver, but it is usually felt at the higher elevations. Don't overdo the amount of exercise until your body adjusts, usually after a day or two. Good sun protection is essential, as Denver and the mountain resorts receive far less protection from the sun's rays than at sea level. Use sunscreen with an SPF rating of at least 15, and wear a hat and sunglasses. Drink more liquids than usual, and reduce your intake of alcohol, as it is absorbed more quickly at higher altitude. When in the mountains, never drink from streams, no matter how clear they look, as organisms that can cause illness are often present.

24-Hour Emergency Numbers

Dial 911 for police, fire, and ambulance.

Rest Rooms

There are public rest rooms in shopping malls and at most attractions. The facilities in bars, restaurants, and at gas stations are usually for customers only.

COMMUNICATIONS

Mail Services

There are post offices throughout the metro area. The main post office is Downtown at 2012 Curtis Street (tel: 303/297-6000), with another branch at 1595 Wynkoop Street (tel: 303/294-4100). Post offices are open weekdays from 8am–5pm, and some open 8am–1pm on Saturday. If you need to mail packages back home, look for the nearest branch of Mail Box, which will pack and ship your goods for a small extra charge. It also offers a Federal Express service.

Telephone

The area code for Denver is **303**. For all calls, you need to dial the full area code plus the number, even for local calls within Denver. For either local or long distance information, dial **411**. For a toll-free number dial **1-800-555-1212**. Many hotels add a high service charge to long-distance calls made from your room. You may save money by using a pay phone in the lobby. Pre-paid phone cards are available at drug stores, convenience stores, and other outlets and are a less expensive way to make long-distance or overseas calls.

To call overseas, dial 011 + country code + area code (omitting initial zero) + the subscriber's number.

Media

Denver's two daily newspapers are the *Rocky Mountain News* and the *Denver Post*. After a century of editorial rivalry, the two papers merged their business operations in a surprise move in summer 2000. The *Denver*

Business Journal is a weekly paper with in-depth local business news coverage. *Westword* is a free, alternative weekly tabloid with investigative news stories on controversial issues, features on the arts and popular culture, and extensive listings. *5280* is Denver's mile-high magazine, published bi-monthly with features, restaurant reviews, and events listings. *Where Denver*, available at hotels, has dining and entertainment listings.

Radio

Denver has several good radio stations, essential if stuck in rush-hour traffic. These include: KOA 850 AM – news and sports; KRFX 103.5 FM – rock music; KHIH 95.7 FM – smooth jazz Colorado-style; KOSI 101 FM – easy listening; KVOD 99.5FM – classical.

Television

Denver has three national network stations: KCNC Channel 4 (CBS), KMGH Channel 7 (ABC) and KUSA Channel 9 (NBC). KRMA Channel 6 is a Public Broadcasting Service (PBS) affiliate. Fox Sports Rocky Mountain is the regional cable sports network.

TOURIST INFORMATION

The **Denver Metro Convention and Visitors Bureau** produces an official Visitors Guide with information on attractions and services in the city and region. To obtain a copy, write to: 1555 California Street, Suite 300, Denver, CO 80202 or tel: 800/645-3446. Website: www.denver.org.

Denver Visitor Information Centers (tel: 303/892-1112 or 800/2DENVER) has three locations where you can pick up maps, brochures, guides. and other information: the main terminal at Denver International Airport; at the Tabor Center, 1668 Larimer Street, and Cherry Creek Shopping Center, Grand Court, across from Neiman Marcus.

Boulder Convention and Visitors Bureau
2440 Pearl Street, 80302
tel: 303/442-2911 or 800/444-0447
www.bouldercoloradousa.com

Winter Park Resort
PO Box 36, 80482
Tel: 800/729-5813

www.winterparkresort.com
Vail Valley Tourism & Convention Bureau
Tel: 800/525-3875
www.visitvailvalley.com

Tours

Excellent free walking tours highlighting the colorful history of downtown Denver are given by volunteers from the Convention and Visitors Bureau, June–Aug. Time: 2 hours.
Gunslingers, Ghosts and Gold is a humorous, historical walking tour of LoDo. Includes saloon stop. Fee. Tel: 303/860-8687.
Denver Foundation for Architecture (tel: 303/779-9193, www.aiacolorado.org) gives historic walking tours, spring to fall. Fee.
Rocky Mountain Arsenal National Wildlife Refuge, 72nd and Quebec streets, Commerce City (tel: 303/289-0232). Free Saturday bus tours to view eagles, hawks, deer, and other wildlife. 9am–11am.

USEFUL INFORMATION

Travelers with Disabilities

Many museums and attractions can provide access services with prior notice. Advocate Services for the Disabled, 1424 Madison Street, 80206, tel: 303/355-8403 may also provide information.

Travelers with Children

Many of the activities in the itineraries section of this book are suitable for children. Attractions in the suburbs that kids will enjoy include the **Denver Puppet Theater**, 5136 West 38th Avenue at Irving (tel: 303/987-3612); the **Butterfly Pavilion**, US 36 and 104th Avenue, Westminster (tel: 303/469-5441); **Water World**, 88th Avenue at Pecos (tel: 303/427-SURF), a huge landscaped water park; and **Lakeside Amusement Park**, I-70 and Sheridan Boulevard (tel: 303/477-1621).

Maps and Travel Bookshops
Maps Unlimited
800 Lincoln
Tel: 303/623-4299
Offers a comprehensive range of maps, including city maps and topographical maps, and guidebooks covering local to international locales.

Useful phone numbers

For traffic information and road conditions:
Colorado State Patrol: 303/239-4501
Colorado Road Report 303/639-1234

Website

www.denver.org – a comprehensive site operated by the Denver Metro Convention & Visitors Bureau, with information on attractions, hotels, restaurants and events.

RECREATION AND SPORT

Denver has an extensive system of city parks and paths for bicycling, skating, and jogging. The Platte River Greenway runs for 20 miles (32km) along Cherry Creek and the Platte River, through Downtown. The Cherry Creek Bike Path runs from Larimer Square to the Cherry Creek Shopping Center. The Highline Canal has 70 miles (112km) of paths through the metro area.

The Denver Parks Dept (tel: 303/698-4900) has information on over 200 parks in the metro area. There are numerous places to rent bicycles or in-line roller skates.

Half of the land in Colorado is public land, with many opportunities for outdoor recreation. For information on hiking, camping, and recreation, contact:

The **National Park Service**, 112795 West Alameda Parkway, Lakewood, 80228 (tel: 303/969-2000).

US Forest Service, tel: 303/275-5350; detailed maps of each national forest, on sale from Visitor Map Sales, PO Box 25127, Lakewood, CO 80225.

Colorado State Parks, 1313 Sherman, Room 618, Denver 80203 (tel: 303/866-3437). Cherry Creek State Park, Aurora, and Chatfield State Park, Littleton, are two popular recreation areas for waterports and also picnicking.

For background information on hunting, fishing, viewing wildlife, contact the **Colorado Division of Wildlife**, 6060 Broadway, Denver 80216 (tel: 303/297-1192, www.dnr.state.co.us/wildlife/)

Mountain resorts such as Winter Park and Vail are excellent centers for hiking, mountain biking, and other outdoor sports.

River running: The Convention and Visitors Bureau lists several companies in the Visitors Guide and has brochures.

Sailing and boating: Colorado Boating Safety Section, 13787 South Santa Fe Drive, Littleton, 80125, tel: 303/791-1954.

Skiing: Colorado has 28 ski areas, many of them within easy reach of Denver. For more information, contact Colorado Ski Country USA, 1560 Broadway, Suite 1440, Denver 80202 (tel: 303/837-0793).

Spectator Sports

Baseball: The Colorado Rockies play at Coors Field, Blake and 20th streets, tel: 303/762-5437.

Basketball: The Denver Nuggets play at the Pepsi Center, off Speer Boulvard and Auraria Parkway, tel: 303/ 405-8555 (information), 303/405-1111 (box office).

Football: The Denver Broncos play at the new Inveso Field at Mile High Stadium (1900 Eliot Street; tel: 303/433-7466.

FURTHER READING

James Michener's *Centennial* is the most well-known novel about Colorado, while *On the Road* by Jack Kerouac has many scenes set in Denver. Stephen White has written a series of mystery stories that feature a psychologist/detective in Boulder. *Perfect Town/Perfect Murder* is the best of the books about the JonBenet Ramsey case (the unsolved murder of a six-year-old child in her home.)

Right: snowboarding at Vail

ACKNOWLEDGEMENTS

Photography	**Blaine Harrington III** *and*
10, 11, 12, 13, 14, 15	**Denver Public Library**
Front cover	**Colour Library**
Back cover	**Blaine Harrington III**
Cartography	**Berndtson & Berndtson**

© APA Publications GmbH & Co. Verlag KG Singapore Branch, Singapore

Left: Cinco de Mayo parade, Downtown Denver

The travel guides that replace a tour guide - now better than ever with more listings and a fresh new design

INSIGHT
Pocket Guides

Insight Pocket Guides pioneered a new approach to guidebooks, introducing the concept of the authors as "local hosts" who would provide readers with personal recommendations, just as they would give honest advice to a friend who came to stay. They also included a full-size pull-out map. Now, to cope with the needs of the 21st century, new editions in this growing series are being given a new look to make them more practical to use, and restaurant and hotel listings have been greatly expanded.

Also from Insight Guides...

Insight Guides is the classic series, providing the complete picture with expert and informative text and stunning photography. Each book is an ideal travel planner, a reliable on-the-spot companion – and a superb visual souvenir of a trip. 193 titles.

Insight Maps are designed to complement the guidebooks. They provide full mapping of major destinations, and their laminated finish gives them ease of use and durability. 100 titles.

Insight Compact Guides are handy reference books, modestly priced yet comprehensive. The text, pictures and maps are all cross-referenced, making them ideal books to consult while seeing the sights. 127 titles.

INSIGHT POCKET GUIDE TITLES

Aegean Islands	Canton	Israel	Nepal	Sikkim
Algarve	Cape Town	Istanbul	New Delhi	Singapore
Alsace	Chiang Mai	Jakarta	New Orleans	Southeast England
Amsterdam	Chicago	Jamaica	New York City	Southern Spain
Athens	Corfu	Kathmandu Bikes	New Zealand	Sri Lanka
Atlanta	Corsica	& Hikes	Oslo and Bergen	Stockholm
Bahamas	Costa Blanca	Kenya	Paris	Switzerland
Baja Peninsula	Costa Brava	Kraków	Penang	Sydney
Bali	Costa del Sol	Kuala Lumpur	Perth	Tenerife
Bali Bird Walks	Costa Rica	Lisbon	Phuket	Thailand
Bangkok	Crete	Loire Valley	Prague	Tibet
Barbados	Croatia	London	Provence	Toronto
Barcelona	Denmark	Los Angeles	Puerto Rico	Tunisia
Bavaria	Dubai	Macau	Quebec	Turkish Coast
Beijing	Fiji Islands	Madrid	Rhodes	Tuscany
Berlin	Florence	Malacca	Rome	Venice
Bermuda	Florida	Maldives	Sabah	Vienna
Bhutan	Florida Keys	Mallorca	St. Petersburg	Vietnam
Boston	French Riviera	Malta	San Diego	Yogjakarta
Brisbane & the	(Côte d'Azur)	Manila	San Francisco	Yucatán Peninsula
Gold Coast	Gran Canaria	Melbourne	Sarawak	
British Columbia	Hawaii	Mexico City	Sardinia	
Brittany	Hong Kong	Miami	Scotland	
Brussels	Hungary	Montreal	Seville, Cordoba &	
Budapest	Ibiza	Morocco	Granada	
California,	Ireland	Moscow	Seychelles	
Northern	Ireland's Southwest	Munich	Sicily	

INDEX